C000228355

EAST SUSSEX
UNDER ATTACK

EAST SUSSEX
UNDER ATTACK

ANTI-INVASION SITES
1500-1990

CHRIS BUTLER

The
History
Press

This book is dedicated to my father
Tony Butler

First published in 2007 by Tempus Publishing

Reprinted in 2010 by
The History Press
The Mill, Brimscombe Port,
Stroud, Gloucestershire, GL5 2QG
www.thehistorypress.co.uk

Reprinted 2011

British Library Cataloguing in Publication Data.
A catalogue record for this book is available from the British Library.

ISBN 978 0 7524 4170 2

Typesetting and origination by Tempus Publishing
Printed and bound in Great Britain

CONTENTS

ILLUSTRATIONS

TEXT FIGURES

COLOUR PLATES

ACKNOWLEDGEMENTS

Numerous people have helped me with my survey and during the production of this book. I should especially like to thank Luke Barber, Barrie Bassett, Ian Budd, Greg Chuter, Kevin Cornwall, Michael Fairbrother, Chris Greatorex, Peter Hibbs, Richard Hurley, Peter Longstaff-Tyrrell, Ron Martin, Geoff Muir, Lynn Russell, John Salt, Paul Sims, Lawrence Stevens, Liza Stewart and Richard Wells. Sue Rowland prepared the Maps used in this book. I should especially like to thank Rachel for her help and support.

PREFACE

The objective of this book is to provide a guide to the surviving post-medieval defence sites in East Sussex. This period covers all types of site from the Tudor artillery forts and batteries through to sites of the Cold War era. Although focussing on anti-invasion sites, a whole range of defence sites is considered, including barracks and civil defence sites such as air-raid shelters. This book is the result of a long standing-interest of mine in aspects of warfare and has enabled me to combine this with my archaeological knowledge to draw on the evidence, both desk-based and field-based, in an attempt to understand the defensive landscapes of East Sussex.

As well as my own research, accumulated over many years, I have used the Defence of Britain database as a starting point in gathering information. This has to be used with care however, due to the incorrect data held within some of the records. Common problems include incorrect grid references and multiple records for the same site, each with slightly differing information recorded by different individuals. After brief desk-top research, I have visited each site to record the in situ remains first hand, often following this up with further site visits to answer questions that arise when considering the data collected. I have also talked to local landowners, other archaeologists and historians, together with people who lived in the area during the Second World War to collect oral evidence. This has frequently meant that additional previously unrecorded sites (both extant and removed) have been rediscovered. As well as producing this book, all of the accumulated data has been incorporated into a database, which will be deposited with the County and National Monuments Records.

Although this book covers the whole period from 1500 through to the Cold War, there is a strong focus on sites of the Second World War as these are the main sites that tend to survive today. It has also become very apparent to me whilst conducting this survey that the surviving sites are under a great threat and are not always appreciated as being relevant. On numerous occasions I have gone to visit a site to find it is no longer there. To quote just one example which reflects the current state of affairs across the county: in Seaford some 30 per cent of the surviving Second World War sites present in the mid 1990s have been demolished during the last 10 years!

One thing that has become very clear as I have researched this book, is that as I have scratched the surface of each site, new things have emerged and there is much more out there still to be discovered and recorded. This book should be considered little more than a current statement of our knowledge and will be the first stage of a larger survey, which will involve more detailed desk-top research to fill the missing gaps. I know there will have been some sites that I have missed and I would be pleased to receive any information on these.

One of the fascinating aspects of the survey for me has been the interest that many landowners and others have in what these bits of concrete are that they have on their land, and the pride that many of them take in looking after the sites. It has also been inspiring to visit sites and see that an owner is making good and sensible use of a pillbox or other feature in their garden, as this will ultimately help to preserve it for the future. Frequently landowners have been able to provide me with additional information about their sites and without exception have been pleased to let me visit sites on their land and record them.

Please note: the inclusion of a site in this book does not imply that you can visit it. Whilst many sites are on public access land or alongside public rights of way, you should always obtain permission before visiting a site on private land.

1

INTRODUCTION

It is not my intention to provide an historical account of the period, as there are many other sources for this information and the bibliography in this book can be consulted for more general background reading on this subject. However, to put the sites into their historical context, this chapter includes a brief description of each major period during the timeline and discusses the different types of site, explaining their construction and function. The chapter then concludes with an outline of how the book is organised and suggestions as to how to use it to see the surviving sites.

THE HISTORICAL CONTEXT

The Tudor period saw many changes in warfare, with artillery beginning to dominate warfare both on land and at sea. The medieval castle had been in decline for some time and during the Tudor period was replaced by artillery forts and batteries built to protect ports and possible landing places along the south coast. Only one artillery fort was built in East Sussex, Camber Castle (Site 27) (*colour plate 1*), whilst a number of earthen batteries were thrown up to protect ports such as Rye (Site 28) and Seaford (Site 8). The earthen batteries generally comprised a rampart of earth thrown up from a ditch, sometimes with a timber palisade added to the top of the rampart. Cannons were positioned on a platform behind the rampart, the number varying from place to place.

The East Sussex coast was particularly vulnerable to cross-channel raids, with Brighton being attacked in 1514. In July 1545 the French fleet made an attack on the south coast after an engagement at Portsmouth in which the Mary Rose was sunk. On the 21 July 1545 a French fleet was off Brighton and on the 22 a French force landed at Seaford. The wars with France ended when Calais was ceded to the French and during the reign of Elizabeth I wars with Spain led to a shift in focus to the south-west of England. A system of Fire Beacons was used to provide warning of an attack and the coastal batteries were manned during the Spanish Armada threat in 1588.

1 The Seaford Battery, built in 1760. From a sketch by H.H. Evans in the nineteeth century, before its destruction in the storms of 1865 and 1875. *Copyright: Seaford Museum and Heritage Society*

After this the coastal defences went into a period of decline and abandonment. The Civil War had little direct impact on East Sussex, with its population being predominantly Parliamentarian. The only major skirmish took place at Rye in August 1648 when Royalist insurgents attempted to capture the magazine. In 1690 the English and Dutch fleets engaged the French fleet at the Battle of Beachy Head, which the allies lost and retreated to Rye, but the *Anne* was lost at Pett (Site 25).

Throughout this time the Wealden iron industry had been involved in the production of cannon, as well as providing huge quantities of iron for other products such as horseshoes, nails etc. Although there were numerous iron-working sites across the East Sussex Weald, few of these are accessible or survive sufficiently to be interpreted by a visitor today. Ashburnham is included in the book as a representative example (Site 47).

There was very little military activity in East Sussex during the eighteenth century until the last decade when events on the continent sparked a major programme of rebuilding. A number of large forts and batteries (*1*) were built at vulnerable points along the East Sussex coast, including Brighton (Site 1), Seaford (Site 8) and Langney, Eastbourne (Site 15).

The threat from Revolutionary France and then from Napoleon saw the largest concentration of military activity in Sussex up to that point, as defences were put into place and regular troops and militia were installed in garrisons across the county to face the expected invasion. On the east side of the county the Royal Military Canal was constructed between 1804 and 1809, and ran from near the coast at Pett Level (Site 25), passing south of Winchelsea, then past Rye, through Iden Lock (Site 51) and on into Kent. A line of 73 Martello Towers

Martello Towers, Pevensey Bay. 841.

2 Martello Towers at Pevensey Bay, looking west towards Eastbourne. Probably dating from the end of the nineteenth century

was constructed from 1805 to 1808 between Folkstone in Kent and Eastbourne, with a further tower added at Seaford in 1808. The Martello Towers were round brick-built towers, two storeys high, with a cannon mounted on the roof. They were constructed at regular intervals along the coast (2), and designed to be inter-supporting. Of the 47 Martello Towers built in Sussex, only 10 survive today. A redoubt with a garrison of 350 men and 11 cannon was also built at Eastbourne (Site 14), whilst numerous signal stations were constructed at intervals along the coast.

Inland and along the coast, dozens of barracks were built to take the *c.*20,000 regular and militia soldiers that flooded into Sussex. These varied from small temporary camps on the South Downs through to large permanent barracks holding hundreds of soldiers (3). A few were constructed from brick (e.g. Preston Barracks at Brighton (Site 1)), but the majority were wooden buildings with thatched or tiled roofs, and most were sold off and dismantled at the end of the Napoleonic Wars.

After the Napoleonic Wars, there was another period of decay, with many of the forts, batteries and Martello Towers being lost to coastal erosion or neglect. However, in the later part of the nineteenth century a new French invasion scare initiated yet another phase of defence-work construction. The forts at Langney and Seaford were re-armed and a new fort was constructed at Newhaven (Site 3) using some of the latest construction techniques and artillery. Again the expected threat did not materialise and by the end of the nineteenth century the only fortification still in use along the East Sussex coast was Newhaven Fort.

The First World War had little initial impact on East Sussex. However, later there was a huge influx of soldiers into the county, with huge training camps set up on the Downs and inland, with large areas of countryside used for training.

3 Napoleonic Barracks, Bexhill. Painting by Francis Grose c.1804. Copyright: Bexhill Museum

Most of these camps have disappeared from the landscape, but here and there are odd remnants that survive: the occasional building or lines of partly in-filled trenches. There was little fortification of the coast, although Newhaven Fort was re-armed and some vulnerable landing places may have been protected. The cable hut at Cuckmere Haven may have originated as a machine gun bunker in the First World War (Site 11), but this is a rare survivor.

A new form of defence site made its appearance in the First World War; this was the airfield, associated either with aircraft or airships. A number of examples were located in East Sussex, including an airship base at Polegate (Site 14), a seaplane base at Tide Mills (Site 5) and St Anthony's airfield at Eastbourne (Site 14). These were fairly substantial establishments, with hangars, maintenance and domestic buildings, some of which survived at the sites for many years after the war. Today there is little structural evidence surviving, but some remnants at all three bases still exist.

The Second World War brought about the most extensive period of anti-invasion construction work ever seen. There were a number of significant differences from previous defence construction schemes. The first was the move away from just coastal defence sites to a network of defence lines along rivers and other obstacles, as well as the normal coastal defences. Secondly, in response to the changes that had taken place in warfare over the preceding decades, much greater emphasis was put on anti-aircraft defences. Finally, as the Luftwaffe could now bring the war directly to British towns there was a huge effort geared towards civil defence. The vast number of sites built during the war provides us with the best surviving evidence for anti-invasion sites, but it is a diminishing resource.

Most sites were cleared away within a year or so of the end of the war and many others have gone since; unless we act soon to protect the remaining sites, these will also disappear.

Along the beaches of East Sussex barbed wire, mines, anti-tank scaffolding and cubes were laid (*4*), whilst pillboxes were sited at regular intervals. Emergency Coastal Batteries, utilising ex-naval guns from storage, were quickly set up to cover the most vulnerable landing places, whilst schemes for setting the sea alight with burning fuel were put in place. Inland, roadblocks and other obstructions were established at important points, and fields were blocked with poles, cables and trenches to stop aircraft and gliders landing. Stop Lines were set up along rivers across the county to block the routes the Germans would be expected to take towards London. The most important stop line was the GHQ Stop Line, which ran from Newhaven on the coast following the River Ouse northwards and then the line of the River Uck and finally the River Medway to the Thames. This Stop Line was protected by hundreds of pillboxes set at regular intervals along the rivers and is covered in detail in Chapter 3. Additionally, bridges were prepared for demolition and other obstacles put in place. Other stop lines along rivers were also prepared, but generally with pillboxes only covering the road and railway crossings.

Towns and villages with important road and railway communications were designated as Nodal Points and put into a state of defence. Many were encircled

4 The view west along King's Road Esplanade, Brighton *c.*1940. The West Pier can be seen in the background. *Photograph reproduced with the kind permission of the Royal Pavilion, Libraries and Museums (Brighton and Hove)*

with anti-tank cubes, supported by roadblocks, pillboxes, minefields and *flame fougasse* sites, and were expected to hold out against attack for a number of days in the event of an invasion.

There were a number of different standard types of pillbox used, although not all of them were found in East Sussex. There were also many different variants constructed to suit local requirements or dependant upon the materials and resources available at the time. The most common varieties of pillbox used in East Sussex are shown in figure 5. Other forms of defences that survive today include the different types of anti-tank obstacles. Anti-tank cubes, coffins, pimples (dragons' teeth), cylinders and buoys were all used to form obstacles or roadblocks. The first three types were fixed defences, constructed in situ with a root extending below ground, coffins being found at roadblocks and bridges. Cylinders and anti-tank buoys were designed to be moved from the roadside to form roadblocks and frequently had metal poles in their tops for wire entanglements. They were often associated with curved rail (hairpin) roadblocks, the filled-in sockets for which can sometimes still be found in the road surface. Traces of anti-tank ditches rarely survive, as these were quickly filled in after the war. Anti-tank scaffolding on beaches was also quickly removed, but sometimes was simply cut off at ground level so the bottoms of the scaffolding poles occasionally survive. Good descriptions of all of these types of defences are given in Lowry (1996).

Only one airfield was located in East Sussex at the start of the war, although it was not used as an operational airfield until later in the war (Friston – Site 12). During the lead up to D-Day two further airfields were constructed at Chailey and Deanland (Sites 49 and 42). The latter is still being used as an airfield.

East Sussex also had a number of important radar sites that formed part of the early warning Chain Home network across the South East. These continued in use into the early Cold War period, but are all now dismantled and abandoned. A network of Observer Corps posts was set up across the county, reporting in to the Sector HQ at Horsham. Although they were manned for most of the war, they tended to be of temporary construction and rarely survive, despite the fact that they frequently employed suitable existing buildings, which may still survive. Most anti-aircraft gun positions were also very temporary and only those for 3.7in heavy anti-aircraft guns were more solidly built. Unfortunately the only complete surviving example in East Sussex (at Seaford) has recently been partly demolished and covered over on the flawed grounds of health and safety!

Civil defence sites were constructed in large numbers. Public air-raid shelters, generally brick-built surface shelters with a concrete roof, were built in town centres. Sunken shelters were built at schools across the county (6), whilst Anderson shelters were provided to those who wanted them. Many buildings with cellars or basements were also used as air-raid shelters. ARP Warden's Posts often utilised existing buildings, but there were also many purpose-built structures as well. Other civil defence preparations included the

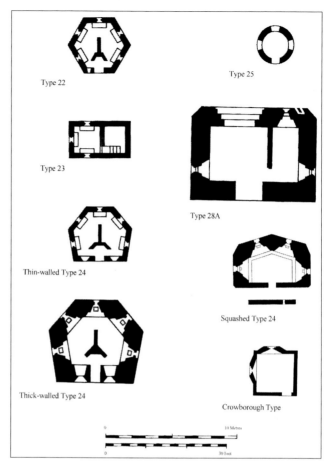

Type 22

Type 25

Type 23

Type 28A

5 East Sussex Pillbox types. The Type 24 and Type 28 were the most common varieties of pillbox built in East Sussex, with smaller numbers of the Type 22 and Type 25 varieties, and only a single example of a Type 23 surviving. The 'squashed' Type 24 and Crowborough types are local varieties with no traceable Type number

Thin-walled Type 24

Squashed Type 24

Thick-walled Type 24

Crowborough Type

setting up of first aid posts, fire-watchers posts and emergency water tanks for fire fighting purposes.

Large areas of East Sussex were utilised for training during the Second World War, with most of the South Downs becoming a restricted area. Numerous firing ranges were constructed in dry valleys for all sorts of weapons, from rifles to artillery. To provide easy access to these training areas a series of concrete 'tank roads' were constructed onto the Downs, many of which survive today as farm tracks. Military camps sprang up across the county and often the buildings remained in use into the post-war period, although now most have been developed as housing or industrial units. There are other types of site for which some remains survive, one being the decoy sites, designed to provide decoys for towns, ports and airfields in the hope that German bombers would attack them instead of the real target. Evidence for this type of site survives at Camber Castle (Site 27) and Alciston (Site 43).

During the Cold War the emphasis moved away coastal and fixed lines of defence to the threat from the air and especially the threat from nuclear weapons.

6 Inside of an
air-raid shelter
at Pelham Street
School, Brighton.
Taken by the
Borough Surveyor's
department, 29
September 1939.
*Photograph reproduced
with the kind
permission of the Royal
Pavilion, Libraries and
Museums (Brighton
and Hove)*

The front line, in terms of any ground war, had moved to Germany and apart
from a handful of military garrisons and Territorial Army Drill Halls there was
little visible sign of defence sites in the county.

   However, the air and nuclear threat was taken seriously and a network of Royal
Observer Corps underground monitoring posts was established across the county,
still reporting to No. 2 Sector HQ at Horsham in West Sussex. Although these
were all decommissioned in the early 1990s many of the monitoring posts are
still extant, although the Horsham HQ building has now been demolished. A
ROTOR radar station was established at Beachy Head and operated for a few
years in the 1950s until its equipment became obsolete.

   Civil defence planning also changed to meet the new threats of the Cold War.
Air-raid shelters for the general population were no longer seen as a realistic
proposition, although underground bunkers for regional and sub-regional seats
of government were established across the country. Instead the emphasis was put
on providing resources for the surviving population after a nuclear strike. To this
end numerous 'Buffer Depots' were established to hold supplies of food and other
essentials.

From the end of the Cold War up to the present day, the story is one of abandonment and decline; with few active military installations now used in East Sussex, redevelopment for housing and industrial units is causing a dramatic decline in surviving Post-War military sites.

HOW TO USE THIS BOOK

There are three chapters in the book, organised to take you firstly along the East Sussex coast from west (Brighton) to east (Camber Sands), then the second chapter follows the GHQ Stop Line from Newhaven north to the Kent border and the final chapter picks up all of the remaining inland sites. I have tried to organise the sites in a logical order and group together those sites that are relevant to one another, so you will find Pevensey Castle in Chapter 1 with its associated coastal sites even though it is situated inland and Lewes town is considered as part of the GHQ Stop Line.

Each site location is multi-period, so covers all the defence installations at the site from the Tudor period through to the Cold War. Some sites have been divided up to make them more manageable (for example the sites around Seaford). Each site starts with a brief historical outline to put the site into its context, explaining what was located there and why. The next section explains what is still there to be seen today and the final section gives directions on how to find the individual sites. Finally where there are specific references for that site they are given within

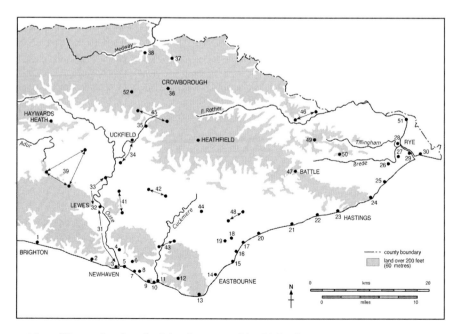

7 Map of Sussex showing all of the sites covered in this book

that entry. The bibliography at the end of the book provides more general reading.

You will find an Ordnance Survey 1:25000 map is essential, and to help find surviving sites, a grid reference is given for each site: eight-figure grid references have been recorded using a hand-held GPS, whilst six-figure grid references are estimated, perhaps where access was not possible. You should note that many sites are located alongside fast roads and in other dangerous locations, so please exercise care when looking for sites. The inclusion of any site in this book does not imply that you can visit it. Whilst many are on public access land or alongside public rights of way, all the sites are owned by someone. If in doubt you should not access a site without specifically obtaining permission to do so.

2

COASTAL SITES:
BRIGHTON TO CAMBER SANDS

The coastal region of East Sussex has been at the frontline of defensive thinking throughout the period covered and therefore it should be no surprise to find that the majority of the defence sites covered in this book are located along the coast and its immediate hinterland. The sites covered in this chapter start at Brighton and progress eastwards along the coast to finish at Camber Sands near the Kent border. Although most of the sites included in this chapter are located on the coast, a small number are situated in the coastal hinterland and have been included here because they have a logical connection with the coastal area.

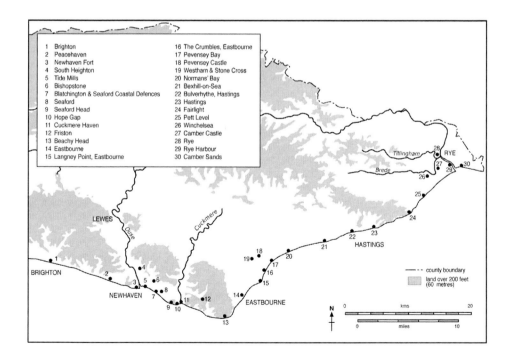

1	Brighton	16	The Crumbles, Eastbourne
2	Peacehaven	17	Pevensey Bay
3	Newhaven Fort	18	Pevensey Castle
4	South Heighton	19	Westham & Stone Cross
5	Tide Mills	20	Normans' Bay
6	Bishopstone	21	Bexhill-on-Sea
7	Blatchington & Seaford Coastal Defences	22	Bulverhythe, Hastings
8	Seaford	23	Hastings
9	Seaford Head	24	Fairlight
10	Hope Gap	25	Pett Level
11	Cuckmere Haven	26	Winchelsea
12	Friston	27	Camber Castle
13	Beachy Head	28	Rye
14	Eastbourne	29	Rye Harbour
15	Langney Point, Eastbourne	30	Camber Sands

8 Map of the coastal area, showing all of the sites covered in Chapter 1

SITE 1: BRIGHTON

Period: **Tudor to present day**
Type of site: **Coastal batteries and beach defences, barracks and**
                           civil defences

History

The earliest recorded defence work at Brighton was a blockhouse that was built on the cliff in 1559 as the town's chief defence and as a storehouse for arms. At the same time other fortifications were erected, which in 1730 comprised a town wall with four gates and a gun garden with space for four cannon. The magazine was situated in the Town Hall. The sea eventually undermined the foundations of the blockhouse and part of the building collapsed in 1748; by 1761 it was a ruin.

A 12-gun battery of 24pdr cannon was established on the seafront at Great East Street around 1760, but by 1786 erosion by the sea had caused its demise. In 1793 two new batteries were constructed; the East Battery was placed at the bottom of Margaret Street and mounted four 24pdr cannon until the guns were removed in 1807 due to undermining by the sea. The West Battery was located in Kings Road, just east of the current Cannon Place, and mounted eight cannon. It continued to be used after the Napoleonic Wars, and was rebuilt in 1829 finally being disarmed and demolished in 1858. An Admiralty Signal Post was established in 1795 on Whitehawk Hill and comprised an 80ft mast and adjacent signal hut, the latter later being replaced with a brick house, built by Mr Pink, a local builder.

At the end of the eighteenth century a number of barracks were built at Brighton, although those at West Street and East Street were decommissioned in 1802, and the barracks at Windsor Street and a hospital in Church Street were sold in 1815. A large barracks was constructed on the Lewes Road at Preston, initially as a cavalry barracks utilising timber buildings, but later becoming an infantry barracks with more substantial brick buildings. Numerous units were also encamped on the Downs around Brighton during the Napoleonic Wars.

After the Napoleonic Wars Brighton continued to be a garrison town, with the Preston Barracks remaining in use. Drill Halls were established in the later nineteenth century for the volunteer corps that had been formed at this time, including one in Gloucester Road for the Sussex Volunteer Artillery, and another in Church Street for the Volunteer Rifles. Large exercises for the volunteers were held annually on the Downs between Brighton and Lewes, some involving thousands of troops.

During the First World War the Royal Pavilion, the Dome and other buildings were used as hospitals, mainly for Indian troops. An officer of the Poona Horse, recovering from a wound received in France, recorded in his diary visits to convalescing soldiers from his regiment at the Pavilion and York Place hospitals. The Chattri Indian war memorial to Sikhs and Hindus who died at the hospitals in Brighton was established in 1921 on the Downs to the north of Brighton (TQ 3044 1105).

In 1940 the seafront at Brighton was put into a state of defence, with barbed wire, scaffolding, anti-tank cubes and mines laid along the beach (4). Pillboxes were constructed at regular intervals along the seafront. At the east end of the town some seven pillboxes can be seen on a German aerial photograph along Marine Parade and Kings Cliff overlooking the beach between the Palace Pier and Lewes Crescent, where another pillbox was positioned in the D-shaped formal gardens. Between the Palace Pier and West Pier anti-tank cubes blocked the ramps from the Lower Promenade and pillboxes were positioned at the tops of the ramps. Other pillboxes were situated so as to provide flanking fire along the Lower Promenade, whilst a number of pillboxes were constructed further inland in the town to cover road junctions.

One pillbox located in the centre of Preston Circus was disguised as the newsagents 'P. C. Brown'. The disguise was apparently sufficiently real to confuse a Brighton Councillor, who tabled a question enquiring who had authorised the newsagent to set up business in such a prominent location. According to Russell Vernon, a Royal Engineer officer responsible for building many of the pillboxes in the Brighton area, none that he constructed were brick-shuttered – wood and corrugated iron were used instead. He also stated that they were normally built by mixed teams of soldiers and civilian contractors, under the command of himself or an NCO.

In May 1940 the West Pier was requisitioned and closed to the public. Later in the summer, 263 Field Company Royal Engineers cut a 60ft section in the pier between the pier head and the Concert Hall using explosive charges; the pier head was then booby-trapped. The Palace Pier received similar treatment.

An Emergency Coastal Battery was constructed on the top of Dukes Mound in Kemp Town (TQ329035), covering the seafront. It comprised two 6in BL MkII guns and two searchlights, and was manned by 359 Coast Battery of 553 Coast Regiment.

A number of anti-aircraft gun positions were located around Brighton. These included 40mm Bofors guns near Ditchling Road and on Marine Parade. Other Bofors guns were located to the east of Brighton, near Rottingdean golf course, and in Whitehawk Hill Road. A battery of four 3.7in anti-aircraft guns was situated at Roedean pitch and putt course (8 Battery, 2nd Canadian HAA Regiment), while a second battery along with their associated radar was located on the playing fields of Brighton and Hove Sixth Form College (TQ 3017 0550). An Observer Corps listening post was established at Richmond Hill.

Amongst the properties requisitioned by the military was Roedean school, which after being used initially by the Army, became part of HMS Vernon in 1941 and operated as the Navy's torpedo, mining and electrical training establishment. As it expanded, additional accommodation was found by requisitioning St Dunstan's Home for the Blind at Ovingdean.

The local Home Guard unit (10th (Sussex) East Brighton Battalion) had its HQ at 22 Sussex Square, whilst its four companies were distributed across the east part of the town; D Company had its battle station HQ in the Gloucester Road Drill Hall.

The civil defence precautions for Brighton had already been prepared and were put into effect immediately after the declaration of war. Numerous air-raid shelters were hastily constructed in the following weeks. Some used existing structures, such as the basements of shops and public buildings, whilst others, particularly those for local schools, were new covered trench shelters (6). Basements below the Dome and Royal Pavilion were used as shelters, whilst a sandbagged shelter was built against the southern wall of the Aquarium. Air-raid wardens' posts were also constructed across the town, mostly as new structures, but occasionally utilising existing buildings.

The defences along the seafront began to be removed in the latter part of 1944 and civil defence sites quickly disappeared after the war was over. However, the Lewes Road barracks and another barracks in Dyke Road continued in use throughout the Cold War. The Lewes Road barracks were used by regular troops until the early 1980s and then only by Territorial Army units, until much of the site was cleared of buildings. It is now a retail park. The Dyke Road site (TQ301059) continues to be used today as a Drill Hall for the Territorial Army.

The sites today

There is no surviving evidence for the early gun batteries and barracks. Some buildings survive at Preston Barracks in Lewes Road (TQ324065), although these are rapidly disappearing through redevelopment. Drill Halls survive in Gloucester Road, where the preserved façade of the Sussex Volunteer Artillery Drill Hall can be seen (TQ 3126 0470), and at the west end of Church Street, where the Volunteer Rifles Drill Hall is located (TQ 3095 0448).

There is little evidence surviving for the extensive seafront defences of the Second World War. A small pillbox is located near the West Pier on the Lower Promenade at TQ 3036 0407. It has been designed to blend in with the adjacent buildings and appears to be of brick construction with a pebble-dashed outer surface and a concrete roof. It has a single embrasure facing east along the Lower Promenade (9). Further east a ramp leads from the Lower Promenade onto Kings Road, opposite the Old Ship Hotel. A wartime photograph shows the ramp blocked by an anti-tank cube and a pillbox positioned at the top of the ramp (TQ 3097 0392), although nothing survives today.

Although probably not in their original location, 29 anti-tank buoys line the edge of Madeira Drive from TQ 3256 0357 to TQ 3262 0350 at regular 3m intervals between the road and the narrow gauge railway line.

Some of the air-raid shelters built at various schools in Brighton still survive, with extant examples at Varndean Sixth Form College, Whitehawk Primary School, Downs School in Ditchling Road and Stanford Junior School. The shelter at Whitehawk Primary School is a large covered trench shelter extending for about 100m within a bank to the rear of the school. It has been restored and is used as an educational resource (10). In 1939 when these shelters were being built, the Borough Surveyor's department photographed many of them in various states of construction and the resulting images are available online at the Brighton and Hove Museums website.

Above: 9 Small pillbox
incorporated into the
buildings on the Lower
Promenade at the West Pier,
Brighton

Right: 10 Interior of the
renovated air-raid shelter at
Whitehawk Primary School,
Brighton

Directions and access

The sites along the seafront can be visited at any time, with the pillbox at the West
Pier located beside the steps down from Kings Road to the Lower Promenade on
the east side of the kiosk. The anti-tank buoys can be found about half-way along
Madeira Drive, close to the road down from Marine Parade.

The only school air-raid shelter that is currently accessible is the one located at
Whitehawk Primary School. Visits can be arranged by contacting the Premises
Manager at the School.

The Chattri Indian war memorial can be reached on footpaths from a number
of different locations, with suitable starting points being Clayton Windmills or
Ditchling Beacon.

Brighton and Hove Museums: Telephone: 01273 292882

References/Background reading

Gray, F. 1998, *Walking on Water: The West Pier Story*, The Brighton West Pier Trust

Goodwin, J.E. 1985, *The Military Defence of West Sussex*, Midhurst, Middleton Press

Goodwin, J.E. 2000, *Military Signals from the South Coast*, Midhurst, Middleton
    Press

Grant, R.C. Undated, *The Brighton Garrison 1793-1900*, Brighton, A Layman's
    Publication

Grimshaw, R. 1986, *Indian Cavalry Officer 1914-15*, Tunbridge Wells, Costello
    Publishers Ltd

Longstaff-Tyrrell, P. 2000, *Front-Line Sussex*, Stroud, Sutton Publishing Ltd

Longstaff-Tyrrell, P. 2002, *Barracks to Bunkers*, Stroud, Sutton Publishing Ltd

Mace, M.F. 2002, *A Suitable Disguise: Camouflage Officers at work in Sussex*, Aldis 71,
    UK Fortifications Club

Rowland, D. 1997, *The Brighton Blitz*, Seaford, S.B. Publications

Rowland, D. 2001, *Coastal Blitz*, Seaford, S.B. Publications

Salzman, L.F. (ed) 1940, *Victoria County History of the Counties of England: Sussex*
    Vol.7, 245-6, Oxford University Press

Various, 1990, *Brighton Behind the Front*, Queenspark Books and the Lewis Cohen
    Urban Studies Centre at Brighton Polytechnic

www.virtualmuseum.info/collections/themes/brighton_photos/html/ww2_
brighton.html

Drury, T. 2005, An Account of HMS Vernon (R), www.royalnavyresearcharchive.
org.uk/Vernon

ESCC SMR: TQ30SW16 – MES189

SITE 2: PEACEHAVEN

Period: **Second World War**
Type of site: **Landing ground, radar site and heavy anti-aircraft battery**

History

In 1917 a landing ground was established at Telscombe Cliffs (approximately TQ406017) to counter possible Zeppelin raids along the south coast and was initially manned by a flight of No. 78 Squadron. In 1918 No. 514 Flight was formed to fly anti-submarine patrols until its closure in early 1919. The initial Bessoneaux hangars were replaced with two wooden aeroplane sheds and there was a Guard House and some Armstrong huts.

A radar site was established on the cliff top, near Chene Gap on Peacehaven Heights, early in the Second World War to provide target and range information for the guns at Newhaven Fort and the Emergency Coast Batteries at Brighton and Newhaven. The site comprised the radar equipment, control room and an observation bunker near to the cliff edge (*11*), and further back were other buildings including an engine house, a transformer house and four domestic buildings. After the war the site continued in use as a communications test site for the Ministry of Technology.

Located to the north of the radar site was an anti-aircraft gun position. The site appears to have had both 3.7in HAA guns and 40mm Bofors guns co-located, whilst a twin machine gun position was apparently situated close to the cliff edge. A searchlight and a barrage balloon position were located at High View Lodge.

11 Peacehaven anti-aircraft battery, a surviving shelter associated with one of the 3.7in HAA gun positions, located to the north of the radar station

The sites today

After the closure of the landing ground in 1919 the site reverted to farmland and is now covered by a housing estate on the edge of Peacehaven town.

Due to recent cliff erosion very little remains of the radar site and all remaining buildings on the site were demolished by 2001. On the cliff edge is a fragment of a concrete base, which is the only remnant of the radar site. Four large concrete fence posts mark the compound around the site (TQ 4306 0023), whilst the concrete bases of two domestic buildings can be found amongst the undergrowth further north. In the centre is a fenced compound containing a modern electricity sub-station on the site of the original transformer house.

A short distance north of the radar site the remains of part of the anti-aircraft battery can be seen (TQ 4305 0051). The remains of two concrete gun emplacements (probably for 3.7in HAA guns) are still present, together with their associated shelters, one being part corrugated-iron construction. The remainder of the battery was located on the site of the caravan park and has been demolished.

Directions and access

Turn off the A259 at the small garden centre on the east side of Peacehaven and follow the bridleway east past the caravan park. Take the small path on the right immediately after the caravan park and you will pass the remains of the anti-aircraft battery on your left. Continue along this path towards the cliff edge to find the radar site.

References/Background reading

Ashworth, R.C.B. 1985, *Action Stations 9. Military airfields of the Central South and South-East*, Wellingborough, Patrick Stephens Ltd

Martin, R. 2001, *Report on Radar Stations at Friar's Bay, Peacehaven*, Unpublished report

Rowland, D. 2001, *Coastal Blitz*, Seaford, S.B. Publications

SITE 3: NEWHAVEN FORT

Period: **Nineteenth century to Second World War**
Type of site: **Coastal defence fort and gun batteries**

History

During the sixteenth century the original mouth of the River Ouse at Seaford became blocked and a new course was opened up in its present location. Newhaven was first mentioned in 1566, and in 1587 it was reported that 'ordnance at Newhaven are unmounted and of little worth'. It was recommended that a bulwark for one demi-culverin and two sakers be raised. In 1596 additional guns

12 Newhaven Town Battery: this lunette battery was constructed in 1855 and mounted six 68pdr guns. Two of the gun positions can be seen, together with some covered magazines. Taken from Newhaven Fort

were provided; however a seventeenth-century map of Newhaven shows cannon barrels scattered on the foreshore.

In 1759 a battery was constructed on the east side of Castle Hill, overlooking the mouth of the river, comprising a parapet, powder magazine, storeroom and barrack, and in 1761 it was equipped with five 12pdr guns. By 1779 the guns were 18pdrs and the parapet was reported as being 18ft thick. In 1801 the battery was equipped with eight 24pdrs and was protected by 200 soldiers, but by 1806 it had four unmanned 24pdrs and in 1817 was to be dismantled except for two guns.

In 1854 the battery had been re-equipped to comprise eight 24pdrs en-barbette and became the 'Upper Battery' in 1855 when a new 'Town Battery' was constructed at the base of the cliff to defend the harbour. The Town Battery was a lunette battery and comprised six 68pdr guns, covered magazines and a barracks for 15 men (12).

Newhaven Fort was constructed in 1864-5 on the east end of Castle Hill, overlooking the harbour entrance. It was carefully designed to blend into the hill and was the first military fortification in Britain to use concrete. The fort was built from brick, using a mix of locally produced red and yellow bricks to create 'pleasing patterns'. On the south and east sides the fort is protected by sheer cliffs, whilst on the remaining two sides a dry moat 40ft wide was constructed. The ditch was revetted with concrete and protected by two counterscarp galleries, the first on the north-west corner with a field of fire along both arms of the ditch. The second gallery was built into the southern end of the western ditch with a field of fire along the southern wall. The entrance was in the north-east corner and was reached using a drawbridge over the ditch. The fort was armed with three 10in RML, six 9in RML, all en-barbette, and two 9in RML on Moncrieff carriages, all of which faced seaward. On the landward side was a single 64pdr RML in a Haxo Casemate in the north-west corner and two 13in mortars.

The Old Upper Battery continued to be armed with four 68pdr guns and was connected to the fort by a passage, whilst the Town Battery at the foot of the cliff was armed with six 68pdr guns. The rear of this latter battery was protected by a caponier (*colour plate 2*); this had its own ditch and could bring rifle fire to bear along the cliff bottom. The caponier was reached by a long tunnel, which descended within the cliff from the fort above. Inside the fort were barracks for the garrison, magazines, a laboratory and parade ground.

In the 1890s there were some changes to the armament, but a major change took place in 1902 when the existing guns were removed and replaced by two 6in BL Mk VII and two 12pdr QF Mk I, with four Maxim machine guns for local defence. The Lower East Battery was re-equipped with two 6pdr QF guns at the same time.

During the First World War the fort was equipped with the two 6in BL Mk VII guns and four Maxim guns which were manned by four officers and 71 men, and two 90cm Defence Electric Lights were mounted on the end of the breakwater. In 1916 a 6pdr Nordenfeld anti-aircraft gun and a 60cm searchlight were added to the fort's defences.

In 1939 the fort had two 6in BL guns (manned by 100 Coast Battery) and two 12pdr QF guns (101 Coast Battery), with the 6in gun emplacements being roofed over with breezeblocks and concrete in 1940. A 3pdr gun was located in the Old Upper Battery for beach defence. Two searchlights were mounted at the base of the cliff in brick and concrete emplacements, and two other searchlights were mounted one on either side of the harbour entrance. A tunnel was bored from the interior of the fort, dividing into two and emerging in the cliff edge to provide protected observation posts (*13*).

Local defence was provided by three brick and concrete pillboxes, one above the entrance to the fort and one each on the south-west and north-west corners. A concrete gun emplacement was located to the north of the fort (TQ 4504 0021). It is partly sunken with an embrasure in its narrower east wall and an access ramp to the open west side. It was probably intended for a field gun, with its field of fire covering the harbour and across the open ground to Tide Mills, but it does not appear on any of the contemporary local defence plans. These plans do, however, show a spigot mortar located in the north-west corner of the fort, and numerous rifle and Bren gun posts around the ramparts. A Bofors anti-aircraft gun was added to the fort's defences in 1942.

To the north of the fort were located a large number of buildings. These included a hospital and other buildings, built during the 1860s, a drill hall/gymnasium built prior to 1928 and in the Second World War a group of buildings

13 Newhaven Fort OP. The Second World War observation post was reached by a tunnel, which can be seen within the fort. The holes in the cliff face are from the shingle hoist used during the original construction of the fort

comprising six living huts, a guardhouse, cookhouse, latrines and ablutions were located at TQ448003.

In 1941 work started on a Coastal Battery to the west of the fort. It was completed in 1943 and comprised three 6in BL Mk 24 guns, a battery plotting room and another unidentified building. The battery was defended by a number of machine gun posts, a spigot mortar and a 20mm anti-aircraft gun, and was manned by 160 Coast Battery of 521 Coast Regiment, who had their HQ at Newhaven Fort. A Type 25 pillbox was located further west along the cliffs towards Harbour Heights.

A radar unit was constructed in 1939/40 on the cliff edge outside the south-west corner of the fort. It comprised a D-shaped brick-built structure, which housed the rotating radar antenna on its roof, and a rectangular brick-built accommodation and/or control building. Adjacent to the latter was a small generator building.

The sites today

After the Second World War the fort reverted to a care and maintenance basis until the disbandment of the Coastal Artillery in 1956 and the removal of the remaining guns shortly afterwards. The fort was sold to Newhaven Town Council in 1962, only to be handed over to a developer to build a holiday camp. This led to much of the original fort being destroyed and houses being built on the Upper Battery. However, the development stopped and by the 1970s the fort was a derelict shell. The fort was then declared a Scheduled Ancient Monument and a programme of restoration was begun. It opened to the public in 1982 and was taken over by Lewes District Council in 1988, with the process of restoration continuing today.

The fort is entered through the original entrance, above which can be seen the remaining 1940s pillbox (TQ 4497 0025). The interior of the fort has been restored, with displays on the history of the fort and other relevant subjects in many of the casemates. The laboratory, magazine and caponier can all be visited, together with one of the 1873 gun emplacements, a Moncrieff emplacement and a covered 6in gun position. Examples of a 6in Mk VII gun and 12pdr QF gun (*colour plate 3*) have been installed in their original positions, whilst the battery command posts can be seen from the outside.

Although all of the buildings located to the north of the fort were demolished after the Second World War, remains of hut bases and some walls can be found hidden in the undergrowth. A guardhouse can be seen at the road entrance to Castle Hill Nature Reserve (TQ 4479 0041) in front of the Pumping Station. The Type 25 pillbox west of the fort was destroyed to make way for housing development. Adjacent to the path from the car park to the fort entrance is the gun emplacement and on the west side of the car park is the entrance to the external staircase into the fort (TQ 4483 0027).

The Second World War Coastal Battery survives almost intact, albeit without its guns, and is an excellent preserved example of a coastal battery. The three gun positions are all very similar, with only minor differences in size and layout (TQ 4471 0011 – TQ 4456 0010) although the central gun position had an integrated OP tower. Each position comprises a circular gun platform, with five ammunition lockers below its rear wall and steps up to the platform (*14*). A further three ammunition lockers are located along each side of the sunken area to the rear of the platform. Behind the gun position is a blast wall and behind this a door to a small shelter. Covered channel ducts in the floor of the sunken area between the gun platform and buildings probably carried electrical wiring to the gun. On each side of the blast wall there are steps and a ramp leading to four rectangular buildings, which provided accommodation for the gun crews and magazines. There is no surviving overhead cover, as it was removed in the 1980s, although metal fittings are still visible on the gun platform and to its rear. The central gun position (No. 2) has had a large blast wall added later on the west side of the position and post-war the OP tower has been adapted for a Coastguard lookout. Parts of the other two gun positions are overgrown with vegetation. To the rear of the gun positions, and now hidden in the vegetation, are the battery plotting room (TQ 4462 0011) and the remains of other associated buildings.

The radar site can be found outside the fort on its south-west side (TQ 4488 0006). All three buildings survive, although the radar building is on the cliff edge.

At the base of the cliffs are the remains of the Town Battery (TQ 4503 0008). Two gun emplacements with iron pivots can be seen, together with

14 Newhaven Coastal Battery: gun position for one of the three 6in guns built in 1943. Note the three ammunition lockers below the position, there are another two lockers on the other side of the steps. Newhaven Harbour breakwater can be seen in the background

their associated expense magazines, while the earth mounds cover the main magazines, which have brick entrances. To the rear of this battery is the caponier (TQ 4500 0012), built with yellow bricks, topped with red bricks and a concrete roof. The ditch around the caponier is now largely filled in. The caponier is accessed from inside Newhaven Fort. There are no visible remains of the two searchlight positions (TV447999 and TV446999), which were both demolished in the 1980s.

Details of the other Newhaven town defences can be found in Site 31.

Directions and access

Newhaven Fort is reached by taking South Road from the A259 in the town centre, which then becomes Fort Road. Turn right into Castle Hill Nature Reserve (past the original Second World War guard post) and follow the road to the fort car park. The fort is clearly signposted from the town centre.

The Second World War Coastal Battery can be found by taking the path in the south-west corner of the car park, past the staircase entrance, uphill towards the Coastguard lookout which can be seen on the skyline. The battery plotting room is to the right of this path, just before the Coastguard lookout, and can be seen by following the narrow original path downslope through the undergrowth. The extant building is on the left at a corner in the path and the base of a second building is on the right of the path.

The radar post and associated buildings can be found by following the dry moat from the car park around the west side of the fort. Take care here as these buildings are very close to the cliff edge.

To find the battery and caponier at the base of the cliffs, continue along Fort Road from the town centre, past the fort entrance and on to the car park (pay and display in summer) at West Beach.

Opening times
Newhaven Fort is open to the public from 1 March to 31 October: 10.30 am–6pm (5pm when clocks go back).
Telephone: 01273 517622
Email: info@newhavenfort.org.uk

Newhaven Historical Society runs a small but very interesting Local and Maritime Museum at Paradise Park, Newhaven: www.newhavenmuseum.co.uk

1 April to 31 October: Every day 2pm–4pm
1 November to 31 March: Saturday and Sunday 2pm–5pm

References/Background reading

Ellis, J. (ed) 2006, *Newhaven Fort*, Norwich, Jarrold Publishing

Goodwin, J.E. 1994, *Fortification of the South Coast: The Pevensey, Eastbourne and Newhaven Defences 1750-1945*, Worthing, JJ Publications

Goulden, R.J. and Kemp, A. 1974, *Newhaven and Seaford Coastal Fortifications*, Heathfield, Errey's Printers

Johnson, C., Saunders, A., Barber, L. and Russell, J. 2000, *Archaeological & Historical Landscape Survey: Castle Hill, Newhaven, East Sussex*, Archaeology South-East, Unpublished Report

Martin, R. 1999, *Report on Buildings at Newhaven Fort*, Unpublished Report

Mason, P. 2007, 'Newhaven Prepares for War', *Newhaven Times*, Journal of the Newhaven Historical Society

Rowland, D. 2001, *Coastal Blitz*, Seaford, S.B. Publications

PRO: WO192/220

SITE 4: SOUTH HEIGHTON

Period: **Second World War**
Type of site: **Underground headquarters**

History

In 1940 the Guinness Trust Holiday Home at South Heighton was requisitioned by the Royal Navy for use as a Headquarters. In May 1941 No. 2 Section of 172 Tunnelling Company RE began the excavation of a tunnel to create an underground headquarters some 60ft below ground, known as HMS Forward.

There were two entrances: the first was in Room 16 of the Guinness Trust Holiday Home, and descended three flights of stairs and through two security gates (the second installed in 1943), into the operations area. The western entrance was situated at the foot of the Downland slope, adjacent to the B2109 road from Newhaven to Beddingham. The operations area centred on the Plotting Office around which were located different communications facilities, including a telephone exchange, teleprinters and a wireless office. The other below-ground facilities included sleeping accommodation, toilets, an emergency generator and an air conditioning plant. Other administration and communications offices continued to be located in the Guinness Trust Holiday Home, whilst local houses were requisitioned as accommodation and a Nissen Hut situated in the Old Rectory garden was used as a Mess. No. 7 Southview Terrace was used as the guardroom.

HMS Forward was defended by an imaginative system of pillboxes, connected to the underground complex by tunnels. Four semi-submerged circular pillboxes, some 12ft in diameter, were constructed from corrugated iron-shuttered concrete. They each had four embrasures and the roof was covered with earth and turf to aid their camouflage and protection. These pillboxes were only accessible by climbing flights of stairs and then finally ascending a wooden ladder into the pillbox.

At the east end of the complex and almost directly above the operations area, a single wooden-shuttered reinforced concrete observation post was constructed. It had four large but narrow embrasures, one on each side, and was entered from the tunnel by two flights of stairs and then a wooden ladder. This observation post was disguised as a chicken shed, enclosed with a wooden shell and pitched roof. There were also nesting boxes with ramps for the chickens that were kept within a fenced enclosure around it. An emergency escape hatch was located in the east wall of the observation post.

At the bottom of the stairs descending from the Guinness Trust Holiday Home entrance, was a grenade pit and small machine gun post with an embrasure covering the stairs. The final defences were located at the western entrance. Externally there was a semi-submerged pillbox of concrete construction with embrasures covering the approaches to the tunnel entrance, with its own entrance independent of the tunnel system. The western entrance was reached by two flights of steps, with access to the tunnel through a gate. The tunnel then turned 45° at which point there was a sentry post with a single embrasure for a machine gun covering the entrance. A short distance past this a second security gate was installed in 1943. On the road to the south of the western entrance was a *flame fougasse*, located on the steep roadside bank.

The site today
After the war the tunnels were abandoned and the western entrance was eventually sealed by the local authority after numerous intrusions by young adventurers and others. In the 1970s the hillside above was developed for housing

15 The western entrance to HMS Forward at South Heighton

and the observation post and four pillboxes demolished with the material being dumped into the access shafts. The Guinness Trust Holiday Home (now called Denton House) was partly demolished and converted into flats. During the 1990s the tunnels were fully explored and recorded, before they were finally sealed. The results of that survey and the associated research have formed the basis of the information given above, which has been summarised here with the kind permission of Geoffrey Ellis. Today, the tunnels remain closed and it is not possible to enter them, however the western entrance and its adjacent pillbox can be seen from the side of the A26 road at TQ 4483 0271 (*15*).

On the hillside above the tunnels some of the original buildings are still present (TQ451027). The remaining part of Denton House can be seen in Forward Close, whilst the cottages in Southview Terrace are nearby and the Old Rectory is located in Heighton Road.

Directions and access
Take the A26 road from Newhaven, and at the junction with the B2109 pull into the small lay-by on the latter road. Walk north alongside the A26 for about 100m to see the western entrance and pillbox. The remaining buildings on the

hillside can be reached by turning off the B2109 into Denton Road to South Heighton. Turn left at the Flying Fish public house into Rectory Road, then left in Heighton Road. The Old Rectory is on the left and Forward Close is the next turning on the left.

Although there is no access to the tunnel today, a virtual tour is possible at the HMS Forward web site (www.secret-tunnels.co.uk).

References/Background reading

Ellis, G. 1996, *The Secret Tunnels of South Heighton*, Seaford, S.B. Publications

www.secret-tunnels.co.uk

SITE 5: TIDE MILLS

Period: **First and Second World Wars**
Type of site: **Seaplane base and deserted village**

History

RNAS Newhaven opened as a seaplane base in May 1917 and was located on the east side of the River Ouse between Mill Creek and the beach (TQ455002). It initially comprised a double-fronted wooden hangar measuring 120ft x 50ft, with concrete hardstanding and a wooden slipway. The officers were billeted in Tide Mills village or Bishopstone, whilst the men were quartered in wooden huts at the base, which were built on piles to avoid flooding. In 1918 an Admiralty Type G steel-framed hangar measuring 180ft x 60ft was erected at the base with a lean-to annex along the north side, together with a second slipway; both slipways were now constructed from concrete, as the original wooden slipway had been damaged. Other buildings were also erected including a carrier pigeon loft and a balloon section base.

The base was initially home to four Short 184 floatplanes, which were later supplemented with a few Fairey Campania seaplanes and three Fairey IIIB seaplanes. These aircraft were engaged in anti-submarine patrols and escorting convoys in the channel through to the end of the war. In April 1918 with the formation of the RAF, the aircraft formed 408 and 409 flights, and were incorporated into 242 Squadron in July 1918. The base was closed in May 1919.

Tide Mills village grew up around the tide mill that was built here in the 1760s to house the workers and their families. After the mill closed in the late nineteenth century, the village continued to be occupied, until the population were evacuated at the start of the Second World War. The village was then demolished, and was used as a training ground to practice fighting in built-up areas, until the troops moved away to carry out this type of training in the bombed-out ruins of seaside towns like Eastbourne.

The beach in front of Tide Mills was lined with anti-tank cubes, barbed wire and mines in 1940, and, according to a German Army map, two pillboxes were located at the top of the beach, one of which may have been positioned at the ruined Chailey Heritage hospital.

Later in the war, the road to Tide Mills was metalled with a concrete surface, which continued through the village and onto the beach, where it fanned out to provide a large area of hardstanding. The beach defences were cleared away and this road was used to move tanks and other vehicles down to the beach for loading onto landing craft for D-Day.

The sites today

The layout of the seaplane base can still be determined at the site, as the concrete bases of the hangars, the hardstanding and the slipways still survive. The original (1917) wooden hangar was removed after the war and reassembled in Newhaven, where it was destroyed in a fire in the 1960s. The larger (1918) hangar was dismantled and moved to Wimbledon, where it was reassembled and still remains today.

Approaching the site from the east, the first area of concrete is the base for the 1918 hangar (TQ 4562 0023). The twin rails mark the front of the hangar, with rectangular disturbed areas marking the site of the buttresses that stood on either side of the door. The rails were to slide the doors open and can be traced in either direction to their stops (*16*). Over the bank to the north the remainder of the hangar can be seen, with further door rails marking the rear wall and annex. In front of this hangar is a large area of concrete hardstanding, with an angled slipway at the east end. The concrete base of the 1917 hangar is a little further west (TQ 4555 0025) and can be identified by the twin rails for the front doors. In front of the hangar doors is a line of inserted concrete blocks with double metal holdfasts, which are probably to secure aircraft parked on the concrete hardstanding. A concrete slipway can be seen on the beach side of the hardstanding.

In Tide Mills village there are concrete bases for two buildings at TQ 4596 0029, which may be associated with the First World War seaplane base; other concrete foundations nearby may mark the location of another smaller building. These buildings were reused in the inter-war period as stables and demolished in 1940.

There is also some evidence surviving for the use of the ruined buildings and walls of Tide Mills village as defensive positions during the Second World War. Two rifle loopholes have been cut through flint walls and lined with concrete (*colour plate 4*). The first is in the west wall of an open yard by the 1930s bungalow at TQ 4594 0028 and faces west across the lagoon, whilst the second is in the west wall of the stables (TQ 4595 0030) with a good field of fire north-west along the lagoon. Located in the allotments at TQ 4601 0029 is a sunken shelter of unknown function, whilst large holes have been knocked through the south and east walls of the allotment area. Whether these are for the emplacement of weapons, or perhaps to allow access during training exercises is not known.

16 Tide Mills seaplane base, looking east towards Seaford. These twin rails mark the position of the sliding doors of the 1918 hangar. The disturbed areas mark the locations of buttresses

Directions and access

Park in the small car park at the west end of Marine Parade. Turn right out of the car park and cross the road, following the concrete path past the Newhaven and Seaford Sailing Club. After 600m you will pass the ruined Chailey Heritage hospital and after a further 100m turn right to get to Tide Mills village, or continue straight on to find the seaplane base. There are numerous signboards around the village giving details of its history.

Opening times
Access at any reasonable time.

References/Background reading

Ashworth, R.C.B. 1985, *Action Stations 9. Military airfields of the Central South and South-East*, Wellingborough, Patrick Stephens Ltd

Fellows, P. 2001, *Newhaven Seaplane Station – A Short History of a local Seaplane Station 1917-1920*, Unpublished, Seaford Museum

1941/06/01 Sheet (Blatt) 134

SITE 6: BISHOPSTONE

Period: **Second World War**
Type of site: **Pillboxes and anti-tank obstacles**

History

Bishopstone railway station is located on the Lewes to Seaford line and was opened in 1938. The frontage of the station was constructed in a typical art deco style, with an unusual octagonal-shaped roof on the booking hall towering above the frontage of the building, and with the ceiling of the booking hall built from glass bricks.

On the roof of the station are two pillboxes, each with two embrasures facing south-east, north-east, south-west and north-west, with good views in all directions. These would have been able to dominate the ground to the west towards the Tide Mills, whilst also covering the railway line cutting on the east side. The two pillboxes are connected by a crawling passage with a sloping concrete roof. There is an opening from the east pillbox onto the roof and another opening, which has been cut through the external wall of the north-west facet of the atrium and has been subsequently bricked up. There would presumably have been a ladder for access internally through this opening. The evidence suggests that the pillboxes were not contemporary with the construction of the station as had been thought, but were added at a later date.

Although the pillboxes were never used in action, the rail network itself was the subject of some German attacks. On 3 July 1940 the 17.37 train from Seaford was machine-gunned between Bishopstone Station and Tide Mills. The driver, Charles Pattenden was killed, but the passengers ducked down and tried to hide under the seats. The aircraft then dropped six bombs nearby which shattered the windows of the carriages and injured several passengers.

There were another three pillboxes co-located with Bishopstone railway station according to a German aerial photograph. One was located on the seafront to the south-west of the station, one to the south-east and one immediately to its north. Additionally, the seafront was lined with anti-tank cubes, barbed wire and other defences linked in with those situated at the Tide Mills (see Site 5) and Seaford (see Site 8). There was also a plan to pump oil into the sea in the event of an invasion and then set it alight (Sea Flame Barrage). A brick-built pumphouse was situated close to Bishopstone Station for this purpose.

The sites today

Today Bishopstone railway station is unmanned, but still open, with a limited train service. Although it is not possible to gain access to the pillboxes themselves, they are best viewed from the front of the station, but can also be seen from the platform, especially at the east end. You can also get a good view of the area dominated by the pillboxes towards Tide Mills to the west.

17 Bishopstone: pump house associated with the Sea Flame Barrage. Inside are two metal pipes, between which the pump would have been placed

Of the other defences, some remain scattered around the area. The most obvious are seven unusual anti-tank blocks situated in front of the Newhaven and Seaford Sailing Club building (TV 4670 9978). Within the Sailing Club grounds (TV 4674 9984) are three anti-tank cylinders and a further rectangular block, all painted white. A fourth cylinder was previously recorded there, but may be the one now in the Marine Parade car park.

Of the three pillboxes, evidence for one only now survives. This is situated on the reverse of the sea wall to the west of the Newhaven and Seaford Sailing Club building at TV 4664 9983. The badly damaged concrete base has a remnant of the lower wall of the pillbox remaining. It is not clear whether the height of the pillbox would have been above the seawall, or whether its field of fire was intended to be along the rear of the seawall.

A rectangular brick-built structure with a gently sloping concrete roof is located beside Marine Parade, close to Bishopstone Station at TQ 4687 0001 (*17*). It has a wide door in its west wall and a window in the east wall, together with three small air vents. Inside there are two large metal pipes that emerge from the floor and turn 90° to face each other. A pump/valve originally stood between the two pipes. It is thought that this was the pumphouse for the Sea Flame Barrage.

Directions and access

Bishopstone station is situated at TV 4692 9993. Turn off the A259 into Marine Parade, then turn immediately left into Hawth Hill and then right into Station Road.

To find the other sites, turn back left into Marine Parade and head towards Seaford, the small pumphouse is located almost immediately on the right side of the road. Continue along Marine Parade and pull into the small car park on the left just after the sharp left-hand bend. Turn right out of the car park and cross the road, following the concrete path along the top of the beach to the Newhaven and Seaford Sailing Club building.

Opening times
Access at any reasonable time.

References/background reading

Martin, R. 2004, 'Bishopstone Station', *Sussex Industrial Archaeology Society Newsletter* 124, 14

SITE 7: BLATCHINGTON AND SEAFORD COASTAL DEFENCES

Period: **Tudor to nineteenth century**
Type of site: **Coastal batteries and Martello Tower**

History

The bay between Seaford and Newhaven had been recognised as a prime landing area for many years. In 1545 some 1500 French landed at Blatchington, but were repelled by the local townsfolk with a loss of 100 men. The earliest record of a battery at Blatchington is in 1587 when 'two ramparts of earth with one demi-culverin and one sacre cannon in each' were noted as being required, but only 'one sacre was mounted and furnished'. Seaford defences were slightly better with 'one faulcon and two faulconets mounted and furnished'.

Seaford Battery was constructed in 1760 and stood on the beach some 700ft to the west of the later Martello Tower, just above the high water mark. This battery had five 12pdr cannons installed in the same year. It was a lunette battery, and had a magazine and soldiers quarters immediately to its rear (*1*). There was also a signal house nearby in 1794. The Seaford Battery was later damaged in the storm of 1865 and again in the great storm of 1875, after which it was sold off and broken up.

A second battery located 'on the rising ground westward' at Blatchington was also started in 1760, although it was not completed until 1761. Five 24pdr cannon were initially mounted, although by 1870 six guns were located there and the site was referred to as Blatchington Fort. The battery also contained magazines and soldiers quarters with a master gunners' quarters located outside the fort. In 1794 12 acres behind the fort were purchased and a new barracks was erected. Throughout the Revolutionary and Napoleonic Wars, Militia units from across the country were based at the barracks and on 17 April 1795 the Royal

Oxfordshire Militia were involved in a mutiny which was put down without violence the next day by regular troops and volunteers.

The barracks were sold at auction in 1818, with three infantry barracks, eight cavalry barracks and two officers mess houses and a kitchen listed in the *Sussex Weekly Advertiser*. The fort was severely damaged by flooding in 1824 and was finally sold off in a ruinous state in 1870.

Martello Tower 74 is the most westerly of the Martello Towers constructed along the south coast. Construction of the Tower started in 1806 and it was completed in 1808. The Tower was provided with a moat for additional protection and at the time of its construction would have been surrounded by the shingle beach. Access to the Tower was by a drawbridge across the moat, which entered the Tower at the second (ground) level. Inside at ground level was the living accommodation and below this, at moat level, was a store and magazine. Beneath the floor was a large water cistern, which was filled with rainwater collected from the Tower turret. The turret of the Tower was originally surrounded by a low parapet and would have been equipped with either a 24pdr cannon or two 5.5in howitzers. It was manned by an officer and 24 men.

After the Napoleonic Wars, Seaford Tower was initially used by the Customs in their campaign against local smugglers, but by 1873 the Tower was in a poor condition and 'in danger of being washed away'. In 1880 it passed into private ownership and was used as a Museum, and in the early twentieth century became a refreshment room and amusement arcade, followed by a roller skating rink. The Tower was requisitioned during the Second World War, although there are no visible alterations from this period to suggest how it was used. After the war it returned to private ownership and is now owned by Lewes District Council.

The sites today

Blatchington Fort, located at approximately TV472994, is no longer visible, having disappeared beneath the Victorian housing development between Marine Parade and Claremont Road. There is also no trace of the Seaford Battery, although the Jubilee drinking fountain in The Steyne is reputed to stand on one of the gun mounts. A cannon barrel, probably of eighteenth- or early nineteenth-century date and originating from one of the batteries, can be found embedded into the pavement and wall at the corner of Crouch Lane and Steyne Road (TV 4788 9897).

Seaford Tower is the best remaining example of a Martello Tower in Sussex. It is in very good condition and access is possible both to the interior and onto the roof. The Tower has been restored almost to its original condition (*18*) and is now the Local History Museum of Seaford. The Museum is located within the Tower and in the southern part of the moat, which was covered over by the esplanade in the 1930s, and records the history of Seaford and the Tower. Access to the roof is by the original internal staircase, where there is a cannon and replica carriage, which gives some idea of how the Tower would have originally been equipped, although the gun is probably sitting too high.

18 Martello Tower 74, Seaford. Completed in 1808, this is the most westerly of the Martello Towers along the South Coast and now houses the Local History Museum of Seaford

Directions and access

The Tower is located at the east end of Seaford seafront at TV 4847 9849. There is ample parking nearby. The outside of the Tower can be visited at any time, but access to the inside and roof is only possible during Museum opening times:

Opening times

Summer: Sundays and bank holidays: 11.00am-1.00pm and 2.30-4.30pm
                 Wednesdays and Saturdays: 2.30-4.30pm

Winter: Sundays and bank holidays: 11.00am-1.00pm and 2.00-4.00pm

Telephone: 01323 898222
www.seafordmuseum.org

There is an admission charge.
Note: there is no wheelchair or lift access to the tower.

References/Background reading

Fairhurst, D. 2004, *A History of Martello Tower No 74 at Seaford*, Seaford Museum and Heritage Society
Goodwin, J.E. 1994, *Fortification of the South Coast: The Pevensey, Eastbourne and Newhaven Defences 1750-1945*, Worthing, JJ Publications
Goulden, R.J. and Kemp, A. 1974, *Newhaven and Seaford Coastal Fortifications*, Heathfield, Errey's Printers

Kitchen, F. 1985, 'The Building of the Coastal Towns' Batteries', *Sussex Archaeological Society Newsletter*, April, 417

Taylor, D. 2001, *A Seaford Sketchbook: The Drawings of H.H. Evans 1849-1926*, Seaford, S.B. Publications

SITE 8: SEAFORD

Period: **First and Second World Wars**
Type of site: **Camps, anti-tank obstacles, coastal and anti-aircraft batteries and air-raid shelters**

History

Two large army camps (called North Camp and South Camp) were established at Seaford during the First World War to house soldiers undergoing training or in transit. The troops were initially housed in bell tents, but wooden huts gradually replaced these.

Seaford seafront was lined with anti-tank cubes, barbed wire, mines and other defences during the Second World War, which were linked to those situated at Bishopstone (see Site 6). An Emergency Coastal Battery comprising two 6in guns and two searchlights was located at TV471995, and was manned by 343 Coast Battery, later replaced by 342 Coast Battery. A small brick-built guard post was situated on the corner of Marine Parade and Connaught Road (TV 4743 9932), and may have originally been associated with the Battery.

A Heavy Anti-Aircraft (HAA) battery was located on the high ground above the junction of Beacon Road with Charlton Road on the west side of Seaford during 1943 and 1944. It comprised four 3.7in guns in concrete emplacements, and was manned by B Troop 583 HAA Battery. The command structures were located to the north of the guns, whilst Nissen Huts and requisitioned houses located in Beacon Road, Charlton Road and Westdown Road were used as billets.

Apart from Brighton and Eastbourne, Seaford suffered more heavily from air-raids than any other Sussex town during the Second World War, with a total of 23 people being killed and 100 injured. To protect the civilian population numerous air-raid shelters were constructed, especially at schools, such as Seaford Secondary Modern School, where concrete air-raid shelters were constructed partly below ground on either side of the school playing field.

The sites today

There is no trace of the two large First World War camps, although a wooden building from the North Camp survived until quite recently. The North Camp was situated near North Way and North Camp Lane (TQ486001), whilst the South Camp was located between Chyngton Road and Sutton Avenue (TV496989).

Very little survives of the Emergency Coastal Battery. One of the searchlight posts is now used as a refreshment kiosk on the seafront (TV 4310 9878), but the small guard post at the junction of Marine Parade and Connaught Road has unfortunately been largely demolished, although it had survived until quite recently. At the time of visiting the site in July 2006, its location could still be established in the corner of the garden of Beachlands Care Home.

Nothing remains of the HAA battery position as the area has now been covered with housing. Some of the surviving pre-war houses may have been those requisitioned for use as billets. At the west end of Marine Parade (TV 4704 9955), some 15 anti-tank cylinders have been incorporated into the garden wall fronting two houses. According to one of the owners, the cylinders were found lying on waste ground at that location some 40 years ago, when it was being cleared for building the houses. At the road junction between Marine Parade and Dane Road (TV 4788 9897) are black and white road markings that were painted to assist drivers during the blackout of the Second World War. The local authority maintains these markings as they continue to be a useful warning to drivers.

A surviving covered trench shelter, originally located at a school, is located beside the A259 road at TV 5025 9935. It has one entrance (now bricked up) at the east end with brick-built blast walls and possibly a second similar entrance at the west end. The whole of the shelter was covered with an earthen bank to provide overhead protection and would have held up to 50 people. A surface shelter survives at the school in Church Street (TV 4823 9902). It is a double shelter with an entrance at either end, together with an additional entrance in the centre (*19*). There are two long air vents along one side wall and a small toilet cubicle is situated at each end of the shelter.

19 Surface air-raid shelter at a school in Church Street, Seaford

Directions and access

Proceed east along Marine Parade from Bishopstone railway station (Site 6) – the anti-tank cylinders are incorporated into the garden wall of two houses at the junction of Buckle Drive with Marine Parade. Continuing further along Marine Parade the site of the small guard post was located at the junction with Connaught Road, the blackout markings are opposite the Beachcomber public house and the searchlight post is opposite Stratheden Court.

The covered trench air-raid shelter is located on the south side of the A259 heading out of Seaford towards Eastbourne. Turn off the A259 into Stirling Avenue, opposite the site, to park. The surface shelter is situated in the grounds of a nursery school in Church Street opposite the church.

References/Background reading

Longstaff-Tyrrell, P. 2002, *Barracks to Bunkers*, Stroud, Sutton Publishing Ltd

Mace, M.F. 1997, *Sussex Wartime Relics and Memorials*, Storrington, Historic Military Press

Rowland, E. 2001, *Coastal Blitz*, Seaford, S.B. Publications

MFN 1278 – Plan of B Troop 583 HAA Battery (Seaford Museum)

SITE 9: SEAFORD HEAD

Period:	**Second World War**
Type of site:	**Practice trenches, pillboxes and heavy anti-aircraft battery, tank track and firing range**

History

The earliest defence on Seaford Head was the Iron Age hillfort, whose ramparts can still be seen today enclosing the highest ground. In 1795 an Admiralty signal post was established 'within an earthwork' on top of Seaford Head and it was later issued with a cannon to signal to adjacent posts in bad weather.

During the 1938 Munich Crisis military training was intensified, although evidence for this can seldom be found. One exception is the group of practice trenches, which resemble a First World War trench system, centred on TV 4993 9831.

The Second World War defences comprised three Type 25 pillboxes and a HAA battery, which were built on the requisitioned golf course. The golf course was founded in 1887 and was requisitioned in 1940 for the duration of the war, that part of it not used by the Army was ploughed up for food production. The three Type 25 pillboxes were situated in a triangle around a large depression on the reverse slope of Seaford Head. They each faced outwards as if protecting whatever was located within the depression, although today it is not clear what that was.

A HAA battery was also located on the reverse slope of Seaford Head at TV494985. It comprised four identical square concrete gun pits each with an entrance located in one corner and an adjacent external shelter. Within the gun pit was a central holdfast for mounting a 3.7in anti-aircraft gun and an ammunition locker located on the inside of each of the four walls. The gun pits were arranged in an arc facing west, with the command post structure to their rear. The command post was a split-level structure with its lower level below ground. Other buildings associated with the battery were located nearby and later in the war a radar set to control the guns was installed on the top of Seaford Head.

During the Second World War numerous rough tracks leading onto the South Downs were metalled to allow military vehicles easy access onto the training areas situated on the Downs. The metalled tracks generally had a rubble foundation and were then surfaced with concrete. A tank track ran from Chyngton Farm at the foot of the Downs up to South Hill Barn, where it divided into two. The eastern arm terminated in a loop just beyond the barn, whilst the western arm headed some 500m towards Seaford Head, where it too terminated in a loop. There was also a passing loop located part of the way along the western arm. The track was constructed between 1941 and 1942, and led up to a tank firing range located between South Hill Barn and Seaford Head. It would have allowed tanks to climb onto South Hill and then manoeuvre along the crest of the hill to different firing positions. A narrow gauge railway ran in a gully from the rear of South Hill Barn towards the cliff edge, with the tank target outline visible at ground level.

The sites today

Today most of Seaford Head is once again utilised as a golf course, and many of the defence sites have disappeared and been replaced with bunkers and greens on the rejuvenated golf course.

Although heavily overgrown now, the 1938 practice trenches cover an area of some 100 sq m, and comprise a firing trench, orientated east–west, with alternating bays and traverses that conform to a First World War design. Some 50m north of the firing trench is a parallel cover trench, and linking these two trench lines are two communications trenches. The trenches survive to a maximum depth of 1.6m in places. When recently relocated and cleared of scrub, these were thought to be First World War training trenches, but a local who had participated in their construction as a member of the Territorial Army in the spring of 1938 came forward to correct their identification.

The three Type 25 pillboxes are all constructed from corrugated iron-shuttered concrete and are in good condition:

1. TV 4923 9825. The entrance is on the south-west side and its three embrasures face south-east, east and north.
2. TV 4923 9819. The entrance is on the west side and its three embrasures face east, south-east and south (*colour plate 5*).
3. TV 4917 9821. The entrance is on the east side and its three embrasures face north-west, west and south-west.

Unfortunately the HAA battery position was partly demolished and covered over with earth in 2004 for apparent health and safety reasons! Although little can be seen of the site today, a visit in 2006 located a gun holdfast and parts of the concrete wall around a gun pit protruding from the ground. To the north of the HAA battery position at TV 4946 9861 is a rectangular building on a concrete base, with the remains of a metalled track running off to the north-east. This building was probably part of the HAA battery, although its original function is not clear today.

Located against the outside of the east bank of the Iron Age hillfort on Seaford Head (TV 4963 9781), is a rectangular concrete building. It has a door at its south end and inside the building there is a raised concrete platform. Located outside the door is a concrete blast wall, which extends across the front and partly down each side. The blast wall also has a door at the front and an integral roof with the main structure. This structure appears to be the engine room for the HAA battery's radar, with the radar itself being located in approximately the same location as the modern radar.

There is one final site dating to the Second World War at the west end of Seaford Head. The brick remains of the Esplanade Hotel can be seen at the cliff edge. At its east end a small brick-built gazebo sitting on the corner of the brick wall appears to have been modified for use as an observation post, including the addition of a 12in-thick reinforced concrete roof (TV 4889 9817).

Much of the concrete tank track onto South Hill survives today. The east loop is intact, although a little overgrown in places, whilst the west arm can be traced

20 South Hill, Seaford: underground control post for the tank firing range at South Hill Barn

some distance before disappearing under the golf course. Nothing is visible of the narrow gauge railway, although the Barn is still there, and an underground control post is situated in the field to the south of the Barn (TV 5054 9750). It appears to have an external blast wall and overhead protection to the entrance, but has been filled in and is difficult to locate (*20*). There is a roadblock, comprising a group of 10 cylinders placed five on each side of the road, beside the Barn at TV 5042 9804.

Directions and access

The sites on Seaford Head can be reached by either walking from South Hill Barn, from the Esplanade car park at the east end of Seaford seafront (see Site 8), or from Chyngton Way on the north edge of the golf course. Follow Chyngton Way through the strange roundabout arrangement to its end, then turn right onto the concrete track up to South Hill Barn (TV 5040 9809). To find the underground control post, take the footpath across the stile on the west side of the Barn and head south-east across the field towards Hope Gap. It is situated on the high ground about 100m before the stile in the corner of the field is reached.

Opening times
Access at any reasonable time.

References/Background reading

Longstaff-Tyrrell, P. 2004, *Operation Cuckmere Haven*, Polegate, Gote House Publishing Co.

Goodwin, J.E. 2000, *Military Signals from the South Coast*, Midhurst, Middleton Press

Greatorex, C. 2004, *Second World War Heavy Anti-Aircraft Battery, Seaford Head, East Sussex*, Unpublished report

SITE 10: HOPE GAP

Period: **Second World War**
Type of site: **Submarine telegraph cable and cable hut**

History

Before the Second World War three submarine telegraph cables had been laid to France from the UK. The cables ran underground to Hope Gap, where they were laid into shallow channels cut into the chalk bedrock on the beach and held in place with concrete. After Dunkirk plans to cut the cables in the English Channel were not followed through, although they were apparently cut near the beach.

21 Hope Gap: shallow channel cut into the chalk bedrock on the beach, with a surviving length of cable

The Western Union cable hut situated near the Coastguard cottages at Cuckmere Haven (see Site 11: TV 5144 9771) was linked to one of these cables (Western Union cable 1900 to Le Havre). After the Second World War a new cable hut situated at the Golden Galleon public house at Exceat (TV 5144 9929) was used, although more recently it has been utilised as a brewery for local ales.

During the war a telephone cable was laid under the English Channel, running from a GPO telephone cable hut at Exceat underground to Hope Gap, and then across the beach in a channel cut into the chalk bedrock. The hut at Exceat is marked on wartime maps as a 'Repeater House' and was manned by GPO telephone staff, with a guard provided by the Army.

The site today

On the beach at Hope Gap four separate shallow channels can be seen cut into the chalk bedrock at low tide (TV 5096 9734). Lengths of cable still survive in two of these channels, together with occasional lumps of concrete (*21*). Looking back at the cliff, a cable can be seen projecting out of its underground cutting close to the top of the cliff.

The hut at Exceat (TV 5131 9936) comprises a brick-walled passage with a small Guard Post on the right-hand side. Beyond this is the entrance, through metal doors, to a tunnel that is covered by a thick concrete roof and then into a sunken hut, which originally contained all of the communication equipment. This hut, resembling an underground Nissen hut, measures 18m x 4m and has a concrete floor with a corrugated-iron roof. At each end of the hut there is a brick-built square vent.

Directions and access

Park at South Hill Barn (see Site 9) and follow the footpath towards Cuckmere Haven. After 400m turn right and follow the footpath along Hope Bottom to Hope Gap. Descend the stairs onto the beach to see the cables. Beware: there is no other exit from the beach.

To find the hut at Exceat, follow the path alongside the A259 towards Seaford from the Golden Galleon public house for 100m, where the entrance can be seen on the opposite side of the road. Although it is possible to see the Guard Post and entrance, a padlocked gate blocks access to the interior.

References/Background reading

Longstaff-Tyrrell, P. 2004, *Operation Cuckmere Haven*, Polegate, Gote House Publishing Co.

SITE 11: CUCKMERE HAVEN

Period: **Napoleonic and Second World War**
Type of site: **Barracks, pillboxes and anti-tank obstacles**

History

During the Napoleonic Wars two barracks were situated at Cuckmere Haven. The first was located on the west side of the river close to the coastguard cottages, whilst the second was on the east side of the river between Cliff End and Foxhole Farm (TV 5207 9793). This latter barracks comprised a pair of officers' buildings, four soldiers' huts, a pair of magazines and the barrack-masters house. In 1816 they were auctioned off and removed.

The cable hut on the west side of the river, near to the coastguard cottages (TV 5144 9771) may have originated as a machine gun bunker during the First World War. Prior to the Second World War it was used by Western Union as a cable hut for the submarine cable that can be seen at Hope Gap (see Site 10). During the war all its equipment was removed and it was later used as a target, being almost totally destroyed.

Most of the visible defence works at Cuckmere Haven date from the Second World War. On the west side of the river there was an anti-tank wall built against an earthen embankment. It comprises 18 corrugated iron-shuttered concrete blocks, each 4ft wide, set on a concrete base to form a continuous 'crenulated' wall, with the two blocks at the west end turned at 90° towards the sea. These last two blocks are the only survivors of a line that continued the wall down to the sea near the Coastguard cottages. It continues eastwards as a solid concrete wall, covering some 80m in total. Immediately north of the wall is an anti-tank ditch, possibly utilising an existing watercourse. A pillbox was located on the west of the beach near the coastguard cottages and then a further five pillboxes were located along the lower edge of the Downs between the beach and Exceat Bridge, where there was also a roadblock and two further pillboxes. These latter pillboxes were probably Type 24 pillboxes; the one adjacent to the Golden Galleon public house faced east across the valley. There was also a row of anti-tank pimples on the east side of the river protecting the flank of the roadblock.

On the east side of the river at Cuckmere Haven there was an anti-tank ditch that ran east–west north of the beach, from Cliff End to the road onto the beach (*colour plate 6*). At this point there was a roadblock, and then beyond that a line of 20 anti-tank cubes continued the line of the anti-tank ditch to the river. Two pillboxes covered the beach frontage, whilst at the foot of Cliff End there was a cluster of six pillboxes and bunkers. These covered the anti-tank ditch and the area of open ground behind it. Two further pillboxes were located on the lower slopes of the Downs further north towards Exceat.

It is also recorded that a pair of 18/25pdr guns were positioned here, and two possible artillery positions are recorded in the Defence of Britain database. Another source states that a single 13pdr gun was located at TV 515 977. Additional beach defences included barbed wire and minefields.

According to Russell Vernon, at that time a Lieutenant in the Royal Engineers who had served with the BEF in France, he was given full authority by his commanding officer to decide where each pillbox should be located and which type of pillbox to construct. He then indented for the necessary materials and used his own men and civilian contractors to complete the task.

Between 1942 and 1943 Cuckmere Haven was used as a QL decoy site. This involved the installation of lighting to represent the lights of factories, railway yards and other activities, to distract German bombers away from the real target at Newhaven.

The sites today

Very little of the Napoleonic barracks survives on the eastern side of the river. However at TV 5207 9793 a circular concrete water reservoir 3m in diameter and standing 1m high, together with its associated concrete trough can be seen. A similar reservoir also survives on the west side of the river.

The cable hut was renovated by its owners after the Second World War and is now used as a fisherman's hut.

On the west of the river the anti-tank wall (TV 5148 9775) and ditch survive to the north of the beach. On the beach itself, below the coastguard cottages, are a number of uprooted anti-tank blocks (TV 5142 9764), one of which has been incorporated into the recently constructed cliff defences. The pillbox next to the coastguard cottages was demolished in the 1980s, but photographic evidence shows it to have been an unusual brick-shuttered Type 24, with a very thick concrete roof, which had chamfered edges. A pillbox survives just north of the beach along the Vanguard Way at TV 5142 9776. It is 4m sq, constructed of brick-shuttered concrete with a concrete roof. It has steps descending into it from the north side and an embrasure in its south-east corner, providing a field of fire across the beach. All the remaining pillboxes on the west side of the river appear to have been destroyed.

To the east of the river the anti-tank ditch can still be determined, especially at its east end. The row of 20 anti-tank cubes is set side-by-side against an earthen bank at TV 5164 9784 (*colour plate 7*). The easternmost cube has contemporary graffiti inscribed into the cement '133 COY, 3 SECT'. Three Section of 133 Company, Auxiliary Military Pioneer Corps were engaged on anti-tank defence work between June 1940 and January 1941. This inscription is now difficult to read, but similar graffiti can be found on some of the other cubes. Nothing remains of the three pillboxes that were located close to the beach, but along the lower slopes of Cliff End five pillboxes and emplacements survive.

Closest to the beach, and covering the anti-tank ditch, is a Type 23 pillbox of brick-shuttered concrete construction (TV 5213 9769). Internally it is painted a light green colour and its embrasures retain their wooden framework. A little further north (TV 5213 9771) is an unusual gun emplacement (*22*). This is constructed from corrugated iron-shuttered concrete with internal brick shuttering. On its north-east side there are five steps, possibly originally enclosed in a brick porch, leading down to an entrance. The emplacement has a single large embrasure in the south-west corner, with a brick and concrete shelf support inside. The weapon's mounting (holdfast) appears to be external, located immediately in front of the embrasure.

22 Cuckmere Haven: gun emplacement at TV 5213 9771 at the east end of the beach. Corrugated iron-shuttered concrete construction with an external holdfast in front of the embrasure

Following the slope of Cliff End further north-west, there is a small emplacement built into the lower slope at TV 5213 9777. It is constructed from pre-cast concrete blocks with a reinforced concrete roof. It has an entrance on its west side and a small window, partly blocked with bricks, in its south-east corner. This is probably not a pillbox, but may instead be associated with the QL decoy site. Further west and on top of the slope are two more pillboxes. The first is a machine gun emplacement, probably for a Vickers machine gun, at TV 5210 9783 constructed from corrugated iron-shuttered concrete, with internal brick shuttering. It has an entrance with steps at its north corner, and appears to have some internal wooden fittings, although these may be modern. The embrasure faces west across the open ground, but is bricked up, and the entrance is shut with a locked gate. A few metres to its north is a Type 25 pillbox, positioned to protect the rear of this emplacement (*front cover*). Its door is on the west side and its three embrasures face upslope, although the middle one (which has no real field of fire) is blocked off. There is an in-filled trench connecting this pillbox with its neighbour.

Immediately below the emplacement at TV 5210 9783 are the concrete bases of two small rectangular buildings. They are built against the low cliff and have steps at the east end. There is no indication as to their purpose; they may have provided accommodation for troops manning the defences, as their location would have ensured that they did not obscure any fields of fire, or perhaps they were associated with the later decoy site.

23 Cuckmere Haven: Type 25 pillbox at TV 5211 9924, looking out across the river valley

The final surviving pillbox is located on the slope above the track to Cuckmere Haven at TV 5211 9924. It is a Type 25 pillbox of corrugated iron-shuttered concrete construction with its embrasures covering the track and river valley (*23*). It is in good condition and has recently been underpinned with a new matching concrete base. Norman MacKenzie was involved in the construction of this pillbox in 1940. His recollections were that an NCO and three men from the Royal Engineers were responsible for its construction, assisted by two civilians. The entire structure was constructed on site, with no pre-fabricated parts, and took between four and five days to complete. Construction should have been quicker, but with shortages of cement and other supplies, materials had to be requisitioned from Eastbourne builders Louis G. Ford, which led to delays. The correct corrugated-iron shuttering was also missing, so in the end they used the roof sheets from an Anderson shelter instead.

Directions and access

To access the sites on the east of the river, there is a (pay and display) car park at Exceat on the A259. Take the footpath along the track to Cuckmere Haven, which is reached after a 25-minute walk. For the sites on the west side of the river, either park at South Hill Barn, Seaford (see Site 9) and walk down to Cuckmere Haven from there, or park at Exceat and walk along the A259 to the Golden Galleon public house then take the footpath south along the west bank of the river.

References/Background reading

Longstaff-Tyrrell, P. 2000, *Front-Line Sussex*, Stroud, Sutton Publishing Ltd

Longstaff-Tyrrell, P. 2004, *Operation Cuckmere Haven*, Polegate, Gote House Publishing Co.

Hibbs, P. 2006, www.pillbox.org.uk/concrete_evidence

SITE 12: FRISTON

Period: **Second World War**
Type of site: **Airfield**

History

The first military use of Friston airfield was in 1936, when it was used as a training ground by Nos 2 and 4 Squadrons RAF. It was classified as an Emergency Landing Ground (ELG) in 1940 and Gayles Farm together with a large part of Exceat Farm were requisitioned. During the Battle of Britain Friston was upgraded to a satellite airfield, although no fighter aircraft were actually based there. In May 1941 Lysanders from No. 225 Squadron at Shoreham were using Friston and over the following winter it was upgraded with a watch office, blister hangars and accommodation blocks being built. In 1942 Nos 32 and 253 squadrons, operating

Hurricanes, were based at Friston and took part in the Dieppe Raid operations. These squadrons left after the operation had finished and it was not until May 1943 that No. 41 Squadron arrived with its Spitfires. This and other squadrons continued to use Friston through to early 1945, when it was downgraded back to an ELG, and finally decommissioned on 8 April 1946.

There were two runways at Friston, the main runway orientated north-east to south-west between Exceat New Barn and Haven Brow, whilst a smaller north–south orientated runway was located to the west of Gayles Farm. The personnel were mostly accommodated in tents, with The Gayles being used as the Station Headquarters until it caught fire in December 1943. Other existing buildings at Gayles and nearby farms were utilised, and new buildings and facilities were erected alongside the main road (A259) and elsewhere around the airfield. Two pillboxes were located alongside the approach road to Gayles, facing across the airfield to provide defence in the case of a ground attack.

The airfield was defended by a number of anti-aircraft gun sites, including one position at Haven Brow overlooking Cuckmere Haven, and a number of 40mm Bofors guns distributed around the airfield. The Luftwaffe never subjected the airfield to heavy attack, even when it was briefly designated a 'K' site decoy airfield, with numerous dummy Spitfires, in 1942. However, later in 1942 the airfield was hit by the first of a handful of hit and run raids, which flattened a newly erected blister hangar. The last raid was in May 1944. During Operation Diver two RAF Regiment light anti-aircraft squadrons (2792 and 2803) were based at Friston.

The site today

After the airfield had been handed back to its owners in 1946, it was used for a number of years by the Southdown Gliding Club. In 1988 Spitfires once again landed on the grass runways during the filming of the TV series 'Piece of Cake' after which it reverted back to farmland.

A significant number of installations survive around Friston airfield. The concrete road from the A259 to Gayles Farm and other roads around the farm were originally laid out during the war. Hidden in trees alongside the approach road to Gayles are two semi-sunken pillboxes, some 50m apart (TV 5399 9821 and TV 5392 9814). They are of an unusual six-sided type, resembling a squashed Type 24 pillbox, and are constructed from brick-shuttered concrete with a concrete roof. They are entered by descending steps and then through an entrance in the long rear wall (one pillbox still has its metal door in situ). Each pillbox has two embrasures, which face west and south-west across the airfield, and still retain their metal weapon fittings. There is no internal blast wall.

Situated between the two pillboxes alongside the road are two parallel blast walls, 10m long and 5m apart. It is unclear what purpose they originally served. To the rear of Gayles Farm at TV 5389 9795, are two semi-sunken air-raid shelters (*24*) and adjacent to the cottages is a 1930s building (now called The Stables), which was used as the airfield fire station (TV 5388 9802). This building has large

24 Friston Airfield: the semi-sunken air-raid shelters located alongside a concrete road and to the rear of Gayles Farm

folding doors at ground level allowing vehicle access and accommodation above with a metal stair access to the rear. Situated immediately behind The Stables is a small rectangular brick building with a concrete roof and a large entrance on its west side (TV 5391 9819). It is not clear what purpose this building served, but it resembles a small mortuary and ambulance garage; often found on airfields. Between these buildings and the airfield is an area of concrete hardstanding, enclosed on three sides by sections of pre-formed curved concrete walling and incorporating two small brick buildings on the west side (TV 5384 9797). This may be a fuel or ammunition area, protected by a blast wall, with the brick buildings possibly added later, although the 1947 map of RAF Friston does not show any structure at this location.

In woodland to the south of The Gayles are two bays that have been terraced into the valley side and enclosed by single width brick walls (TV 538978). The largest bay is some 60ft long and 22ft wide with small entrances in its east and south walls, the eastern entrance being protected by a short length of external brick blast wall. The smaller bay is 40ft long and 22ft wide, with a single entrance in its south wall. A third terraced bay has no surviving brick wall associated with it, but has a metal standpipe in one corner. Situated a short distance away is a small rectangular brick structure on a concrete base, which also has a metal standpipe within it. These bays are likely to have been fuel stores, with an associated pump building. A short distance to the east is a single prefabricated Maycrete building

(TV 5408 9781), reputedly used as a hospital. Alongside the A259 road is the base of a Nissen hut, one of a number that were originally located here.

At Haven Brow there are remains of an anti-aircraft gun battery, although these comprise only fragments of brick and concrete walling in a large quarry (TV 5252 9776). This quarry may have held the command post or support buildings, with the actual gun positions located along what appears to be a large lynchet, which has a number of circular depressions.

Directions and access

Friston airfield is located on the south side of the A259 road between Eastbourne and Seaford. There are footpaths from the Seven Sisters Country Park at Exceat, or from the National Trust properties at Birling Gap or Crowlink, although none of these provide access to the site of the airfield.

Unfortunately almost all of the sites at Friston are on private property and there is no public access to them. The exceptions are the remains of the anti-aircraft position on Haven Brow which is close to the trig point on public access land and the possible hospital building which can be seen from the adjacent National Trust public access land (accessed from the Crowlink car park), although the site itself is on private property.

The Stables at Gayles are let as self-catering holiday accommodation and a booking may provide access to the sites described with the owners consent.
Telephone: 07721 023845
Email: contactgayles@onetel.net

References/Background reading

Ashworth, R.C.B. 1985, *Action Stations 9. Military airfields of the Central South and South-East*, Wellingborough, Patrick Stephens Ltd
Brooks, R.J. 1993, *Sussex Airfields in the Second World War*, Newbury, Countryside Books

SITE 13: BEACHY HEAD

Period: **Tudor to Cold War**
Type of site: **Communications stations and bunkers**

History

The earliest signalling post to have been located at Beachy Head was a fire beacon, which formed part of the warning system that alerted the south coast defences when the Spanish Armada arrived off Lands End in 1588. In 1690 the Battle of Beachy Head was fought offshore between the combined English and Dutch fleet under Lord Torrington and a superior French fleet. The warship *Anne* was seriously damaged during the battle and later beached at Pett (see Site 25).

An Admiralty Signal Post was established on Beachy Head in 1795 and was designated a 'Principal Post'. It continued in use throughout the Napoleonic Wars and was later provided with a carronade to alert adjacent posts to a signal in bad weather. By 1803 a military signal post and beacon had been established inland from Beachy Head at Jevington Down. This was a Primary Beacon that could only be lit on the command of the General commanding at Eastbourne and was intended as a signal to assemble the local volunteers and alert other beacons further inland. A map of 'Eastbourne and its environs' published in 1819 shows a telegraph station on Beachy Head, which was likely to have been the new semaphore station that was noted as being 'ready to operate' in 1820.

The Lloyds Corporation operated a watchtower on Beachy Head between 1882 and 1904, with a cottage being built for the signalman in 1897. During the First World War the Coastguard Station at Beachy Head was used as a coast-watching post, manned by Boy Scouts. The nearby meteorological station became an outpost for RNAS Polegate (see Site 14) later in the war.

During the Second World War an Observer Corps post was set up on Beachy Head and, along with the adjacent Royal Naval Shore Signal Station, was strafed by Me109s in May 1942. In 1943 a Bofors gun located at Cow Gap shot down another raider, but the Observer Corps post was attacked again later the same year, its hut being peppered with bullets from both attackers and defenders. At Birling Gap, a few kilometres to the west of Beachy Head, the stairs to the beach were removed, but there were no fixed defences. There is mention of a machine gun post at the foot of Beachy Head, presumably at the east end of the cliffs where it could be easily accessed. The surrounding farmland was used for military training throughout the war, with a tank firing range located near Cornish Farm. The moving targets were mounted on a narrow gauge railway located between there and Belle Tout, which unfortunately meant that the lighthouse was mostly demolished by overshoots or mischievous gunners by the end of the war.

In 1940 a Chain Home radar station was set up on Beachy Head on land requisitioned from the Lloyds Corporation. In 1950 a ROTOR station was built on land opposite the Beachy Head Hotel. The hardened R1 type underground installation was completed in 1952 and the ROTOR equipment to provide Centrimetric Early Warning capabilities was installed later that year. Above ground there was a guardhouse and on a nearby farm a generator house, built to resemble a barn, which provided auxiliary power. In 1954 a new Type 80 Mk1 radar installation was installed, but by 1960 the site was closed and the equipment removed. The domestic site for the ROTOR station was located in Rangemore Drive in Eastbourne.

Just to the north of Beachy Head, a radio transmitter site was established on Willingdon Hill in 1942. The site comprised a number of different aerial types, with the existing Hill Cottages and adjacent farm buildings being requisitioned for accommodation and other purposes. Additional huts and other buildings were also constructed, together with an access road from Friston. Both the Army and Royal Navy used the site throughout the rest of the war, before it was returned to agriculture.

The sites today

Part of the nineteenth-century Lloyds watchtower survives near the cliff edge (TV 5884 9560). It comprises an octagonal brick structure sitting on a brick base, with steps up into the interior, which is now furnished with seating. Plaques on the outside provide information on the watchtower and commemorate the wartime use of Beachy Head. The associated signaller's cottage survived until 1992.

Despite a possible reprieve in the 1980s as a civil defence bunker for local government, the entrance to the ROTOR bunker has now been sealed and its associated above-ground installations have all been removed. The guardhouse was finally demolished in 1996 after serving as a Police house and Coastguard station. The bunker itself is located under the large mound at TV 5900 9579, opposite the Beachy Head Hotel. There are numerous patches of concrete and a short length of concrete road surviving between the cliff edge and the road.

There are some surviving remains to be seen of the Willingdon Hill radio transmitter site. The concrete foundations of Hill Cottages and a number of other buildings survive amongst the trees at TQ 5698 0053. From here a concrete path leads towards the flint walls of the requisitioned farm buildings where further hut bases can be seen. Also noted around the trees are numerous metal stays, which presumably originally secured the aerials. Partly sunken 'Hut A' was located close to the Bronze

25 Willingdon Hill: probable MT shed associated with the radio transmitter site located on Willingdon Hill during the Second World War and situated a short distance to the south of the site

Age burial mounds in the adjacent field, but has been filled in and covered over. 'Hut B' may still be extant at TQ 5760 0085, but is now used as a water pumping station. To the south of Willingdon Hill is an open-fronted brick building with a concrete roof (25), resembling an MT Garage (TQ 5693 0011) and nearby is the base for a Nissen hut. Although these are likely to have formed part of the site, it has been suggested that they were erected for the farmer to replace the requisitioned farm buildings.

Directions and access

The sites on Beachy Head are all located opposite the Beachy Head Hotel, between the road and the cliff edge. There are car parks and other facilities located next to the Beachy Head Hotel, together with a small visitor centre.

The Willingdon Hill site is best approached from Butts Brow car park, which can be accessed via Butts Lane, from Willingdon village. A footpath from the car park leads south to Willingdon Hill. The main part of the site is amongst the trees on Willingdon Hill and the derelict farm buildings (private property) in the adjacent field. The MT Garage is 500m further south along the track.

References/Background reading

Elleray, D.R. 1978, *Eastbourne: A Pictorial History*, Chichester, Phillimore

Elliston, R.A. 1999, *Eastbourne's Great War 1914-1918*, Seaford, S.B. Publications

Goodwin, J.E. 2000, *Military Signals from the South Coast*, Midhurst, Middleton Press

Humphrey, G. 1998, *Eastbourne at War*, Seaford, S.B. Publications

Longstaff-Tyrrell, P. 2004, *Operation Cuckmere Haven*, Polegate, Gote House Publishing

Marsden, P. 1987, *The Historic Shipwrecks of South-East England*, Norwich, Jarrold and Sons Ltd

Surtees, J. 1997, *Beachy Head*, Seaford, S.B. Publications

SITE 14: EASTBOURNE

Period: **Napoleonic to Second World War**
Type of site: **Redoubt, Martello Tower, aerodrome, seafront and civil defences**

History

The map of 'Eastbourne and its environs' published in 1819 shows the Napoleonic defences along the seafront. These comprised a number of Martello Towers, the two forts at Langley (see Site 15) and the Redoubt.

The Redoubt, and its companion at Dymchurch in Kent, was designed to supplement the line of Martello Towers along the south coast. It was constructed between 1805 and 1808, and was built from red and yellow bricks within a dry

26 Eastbourne Redoubt: completed in 1808, it comprised an open central parade ground enclosed by 24 casemates or barrack rooms, four of which are shown here. The Redoubt was built to take a garrison of 350 men and was armed with 10 cannon mounted on the platform above the casemates

moat or ditch, which was surrounded by an earth bank or 'glacis'. It comprised an open central parade ground enclosed by 24 casemates or barrack rooms (26). Above these was the gun platform on which 11 cannon were to be mounted. Within the ditch were five caponiers with embrasures covering the ditch, whilst the only entrance was a wooden drop bridge across the ditch on the north side of the Redoubt.

Ten 24pdr cannon were eventually mounted in the Redoubt, with the No. 1 gun emplacement left empty, having no embrasure through which to fire. In 1812 the guns were put to use, when two shots were fired at a French ship which had strayed too close to the shore – both missed. Although the Redoubt was built to take a garrison of 350 men, it is likely that only some 200 men were ever stationed there at any one time.

Later the Redoubt was rearmed with 32pdr cannon and in about 1860 it had an armament of three 110pdr rifled breech-loaders, two 68pdr muzzle-loaded smooth bores and five 8in muzzle-loaded smooth-bores. Various modifications of the gun positions probably took place at the same time.

The Redoubt was in danger of being washed away during the nineteenth century. Initially a concrete escarpment was constructed on its seaward side, but it was only when the promenade was built that the danger from the sea was finally averted.

During the First World War the Redoubt was used as an observation post, store and convalescent hospital, and during the Second World War it was used as a store, but also had a battery of anti-aircraft guns positioned on the gun platform.

Martello Tower 73 was situated on elevated ground above the beach and the marsh that originally surrounded the Tower and gave it its name: The 'Wish Tower'. It was built using yellow bricks and was surrounded by a moat. On its completion in 1808 it was manned by the East Sussex Volunteer Corps until 1812. Later in the nineteenth century the Tower was used by the Coastguard, and then between 1886 and the 1930s it was a Museum of Geology. During this period it was frequently threatened with demolition.

During the Second World War the Wish Tower was requisitioned, and a two-storey concrete structure was added to the roof and used as an observation post and magazine for an Emergency Coastal Battery. The two gun positions, containing First World War 6in guns, were mounted immediately in front of the Tower, with a First Aid Post located to the rear of the Tower and a Sentry Post on Grand Parade. The whole position was enclosed by barbed wire and a roadblock was placed in Wilmington Square Gardens. The battery Gas Post was located in the south-west corner of the Lansdowne Hotel. The guns were manned initially by 342 Coast Battery, then later by 343 Coast Battery, and finally by the Home Guard.

After the war the concrete roof was removed from the Tower and after further threats of demolition, it was finally restored and opened as a museum in 1970.

St Anthony's RNAS Aerodrome took over the hangars and buildings of the Eastbourne Flying School in 1914 and 17 Bessoneaux hangars were erected, some adjacent to Leeds Avenue, whilst others were erected in what is now Birch Road. A site on the Crumbles, in the region of the present day Sovereign Centre, was used by the Eastbourne Aircraft Company as a seaplane factory and also for refuelling and servicing patrolling seaplanes. The hangars on the Crumbles were converted to an aircraft factory and during the war the Eastbourne Aircraft Company built BE2c aircraft for the RNAS and later Avro 504 aircraft for the RFC; altogether a total of 252 aircraft were built.

The RNAS Polegate airship station opened in 1915 and was operational with three SS-Type non-rigid blimps by the end of the year. Two hangars were constructed, together with wooden huts to accommodate the personnel, whilst concrete roads and a gas plant were added later (TQ581035). Airships continued to use the base up until the end of the war and it was finally closed in 1919.

During the Second World War the beach at Eastbourne was lined with anti-tank cubes, barbed wire, mines and scaffolding to prevent any landing, whilst pillboxes were located along the Lower Promenade. The wooden decking was removed from the middle of the pier and platforms for machine guns were installed in the pier theatre. Barricades were constructed in all of the roads leading from the seafront into the town centre. These comprised beach huts that had been removed from the beach and filled with pebbles. Bofors 40mm anti-aircraft guns were located at a number of places along the seafront, including on the flat roof of the Pier Pavilion and at the Wish Tower.

The Civil Defence HQ was located at 33 Old Orchard Road, whilst the firewatchers used the house built over the demolished Martello Tower 68 as their headquarters. Numerous air-raid shelters were constructed throughout the town. Suitable basements and cellars were also used as shelters, including one in the crypt of All Saints Church. A bomb destroyed one surface shelter located in Spencer Road in 1943 killing some people sheltering inside.

In 1942 the Royal Naval establishment (HMS Marlborough) took over Eastbourne College as an underwater weapons school. Part of the school was apparently located in an underground shelter and Nissen hut next door to Clovelly Cottage in Blackwater Road and Grange Road was closed for security reasons.

The sites today

The Redoubt (TV 5229 9967) became a Scheduled Ancient Monument in 1960, at which time it held a model village and aquarium. In 1977 the Sussex Combined Services Museum Trust was established and a small museum opened. Today the Redoubt is owned and managed by Eastbourne Borough Council and is home to the Museum of the Royal Sussex Regiment and the Queen's Royal Irish Hussars.

Martello Tower 73 (TV 6128 9832) is well maintained and in very good condition externally, despite currently being empty and unused. The moat has been partially filled in and modern steps lead to the first storey entrance. The outer surface has been rendered and scored to give the impression that the tower is constructed of masonry blocks rather than bricks. Nothing remains of the gun positions of the Emergency Coastal Battery, with a café standing on the position of No. 1 Gun. The First Aid Post was located in the building now used as public toilets (TV 6131 9824) and the part of the Lansdowne Hotel used as a Gas Post is located in its south-west corner in Jevington Gardens. The position of the Guard Post is marked by some fragments of brick and concrete that have been incorporated into a wall. Interestingly, two War Department boundary marker stones are incorporated into the wall in King Edward's Parade at TV 6125 9821 and TV 6131 9829 and mark the north-west and north-east boundaries of the battery position.

Little remains of St Anthony's aerodrome. It used to occupy the area to the north-east of Lottridge Drove, now occupied by industrial estates and housing. A single hangar remained until it was demolished by the 1987 storms and its base can still be seen off Leeds Avenue. The aerodrome guardhouse survives as 'The Bungalow' in Leeds Avenue (TQ 6275 0153). It comprises a single storey rectangular building with a veranda along its front (*colour plate 8*); the extension at the rear and its tiled roof have been added more recently. Originally its cell, with bars across its small windows, was located at the north end.

The hangars and most of the buildings at Polegate airship base were demolished after the war leaving only the transport repair shop to survive until 1995, when it too was demolished. Housing estates now cover the area of the base, utilising some of the original concrete roads, and some concrete mooring points survive at Donkey Hollow (TQ575025).

After the Second World War Eastbourne Town Council very quickly removed all the defence installations and began a process of reconstruction and rebuilding. Unfortunately this policy has consequently removed almost all the evidence of both defence and civil defence sites in the town. One surviving site comprises four loopholes in a brick wall in Holywell Close, facing along Meads Street at TV 6008 9729. The steps down to the air-raid shelter in the crypt can be seen on the left side of All Saints Church in Carlisle Road (TV 6088 9831). A Nissen hut that was part of HMS Marlborough survives in Blackwater Road within the grounds of Eastbourne College.

Directions and access
To find the Redoubt, follow Grand Parade east from the pier, The Redoubt is situated at the east end of Royal Parade and can be identified by the Centurion tank parked outside. Martello Tower 73 can be found by following Grand Parade west from the pier, then park in King Edward's Parade and walk the short distance to the Tower, which is set within some gardens.

The St Anthony's aerodrome guardhouse can be found by taking the A259 from the town centre. This becomes St Anthony's Avenue, from which take a left turn into Leeds Avenue. Follow this for 200m and 'The Bungalow', which is private property, is on the right hand side.

Opening times
The Redoubt is open Tuesday-Sunday, 10.00am–5.00pm, April-November.
Closed Mondays except bank holidays.
There is an entrance charge to the museum.
Telephone: 01323 410300
Email: redoubtmuseum@eastbourne.gov.uk

The Wish Tower can be viewed externally at any reasonable hour.

References/Background reading

Ashworth, R.C.B. 1985, *Action Stations 9. Military airfields of the Central South and South-East*, Wellingborough, Patrick Stephens Ltd
Elleray, D.R. 1978, *Eastbourne: A Pictorial History*, Chichester, Phillimore
Elliston, R.A. 1999, *Eastbourne's Great War 1914-1918*, Seaford, S.B. Publications
Goodwin, J.E. 1994, *Fortification of the South Coast: The Pevensey, Eastbourne and Newhaven Defences 1750-1945*, Worthing, JJ Publications
Hardy, N.W. (ed) undated, *Eastbourne 1939-1945*, Eastbourne, Strange the Printer Ltd
Humphrey, G. 1989, *Wartime Eastbourne*, Eastbourne, Beckett Features
Humphrey, G. 1998, *Eastbourne at War*, Seaford, S.B. Publications
Ockenden, M. 2006, *Canucks by the Sea*, Eastbourne, CPI Antony Rowe
McMahon, L. and Partridge, M. 2000, *The History of the Eastbourne Aviation Company 1911-1924*, Eastbourne Local History Society

www.martello-towers.co.uk – Foundation to Firestep – Eastbourne Redoubt
www.eastbournemuseums.co.uk/redoubt/museum.htm

SITE 15: LANGNEY POINT, EASTBOURNE

Period: **Napoleonic to Second World War**
Type of site: **Martello Towers and the Langley Forts**

History

Martello Tower 66 (together with Tower 67 located at TQ644012) was built to
support the six-gun battery of East Langley Fort, which had been constructed
in 1759. It was built from both red and yellow bricks, used randomly. A concrete
roof was added to Tower 66 in 1940, when it was used as a machine gun post.
After the war the Tower was used by the Coastguard, who added an observation
post to the top of the wartime roof. A 32pdr cannon barrel is apparently still on
the roof of the tower. Tower 67 was demolished in 1922 after its partial collapse,
and the next five towers (68 to 72) have all been demolished, lost to erosion or
destroyed in gunnery trials in the later nineteenth century.

East Langley (now called Langney) Fort was remodelled in 1855, and a report
from the Committee on Coast Defences in 1873 stated that the fort had two
10in SB guns and four 32pdr SB guns forming the armament, and a two-storied
defensible barracks on each flank providing accommodation for two officers and
50 men. East Langley Fort was still extant in 1910, as it appeared on the Ordnance
Survey map of that date, but by the 1938 edition only the inland part of the fort is
shown, the remainder having succumbed to coastal erosion.

27 Langney Point: three nineteenth-century gun pivots that were originally located in the
Langley Forts, now placed here to block access onto the beach

West Langley Fort was constructed by 1795 and was armed with six 24pdr cannon. It was sited on the shingle between Martello Towers 69 and 70, and was lost to coastal erosion during the nineteenth century.

During the Second World War the beach at Langney Point was defended by lines of anti-tank cubes, barbed wire, beach anti-tank scaffolding and mines, which were covered by pillboxes and weapons pits. There was also a concrete revetted anti-tank ditch located along the rear of the beach (TQ641011). Most of these defences were removed immediately after the war, but some remained to be recorded in the late 1990s.

The sites today

Although no longer manned as a Coastguard station, Martello Tower 66 retains its observation post structure. The Tower is in good condition with much of its surface rendering intact, although some large cracks are appearing and some pieces of rendering have fallen off exposing the mixture of red and yellow bricks. The dressed stone around the first floor entrance is in very good condition, although due to the build-up of shingle around the Tower this appears to be almost at ground level today.

Tower 67 was demolished in 1922, although its remains could be seen at low tide until recent work to improve the sea defences. Tower 68 was located on St Anthony's Hill (TQ628016), some 1.5km inland, and was provided with a moat. It was demolished around 1925 and the house that sits on its site today apparently incorporates the Tower's base as its cellar. The road surrounding the house was built around the filled-in moat. During the Second World War the Eastbourne Firewatchers used this house as their Headquarters.

There are no traces of the Langley Forts surviving today, the last remnants were revealed during work on the construction of the Sovereign Harbour in 2000. However, three gun pivots (*27*) recovered from the forts are now used to block an entrance at Langney Point (TQ 6425 0102).

All of the Second World War defences that had survived until quite recently were unfortunately destroyed during the construction of Sovereign Harbour. Amongst the sites destroyed were two Type 25 pillboxes situated at TQ644016 and TQ643015. Each of these pillboxes was supported by a pair of concrete weapons pits, which consisted of circular drainpipe sections sunk into the shingle beach. Some anti-tank scaffolding was also noted at TQ644012.

Directions and access

Take Atlantic Drive from Sovereign Harbour (South); at the roundabout with Prince William Parade take the exit for the treatment works and park in the adjacent car park. Alternatively, turn off the A259 towards the Sovereign Centre and then follow Prince William Parade to Langney Point.

The location of Tower 68 on St Anthony's Hill can be found by taking the A259 from the town centre. This becomes St Anthony's Avenue, from which a left turn into Seaville Drive takes you to The Circus, which encircles the original location of the Tower.

References/Background reading

Goodwin, J.E. 1994, *Fortification of the South Coast: The Pevensey, Eastbourne and Newhaven Defences 1750-1945*, Worthing, JJ Publications

www.martello.towers.co.uk
www.pillbox.org.uk

SITE 16: THE CRUMBLES, EASTBOURNE

Period: **Napoleonic and Second World War**
Type of site: **Martello Towers**

History

Martello Tower 64 is situated on a shingle bank on the Crumbles between Pevensey Bay and Eastbourne (TQ 6471 0216). It was constructed from a random mixture of red and yellow bricks, but little is known of its early history. A concrete roof was added in 1940. The roof area was divided into four separate rooms, each having an embrasure for a machine gun. The original door and windows were blocked up at the same time.

Tower 65 (TQ645016) was lost to coastal erosion in the mid 1930s, when its foundations were undermined and it dramatically split in two and fell into the sea.

The site today

In 1910 the Tower was some 100yds from the shoreline, but today the shingle is rapidly eroding with the sea now only some 50m away from the Tower. Recent housing developments around Sovereign Harbour have sprung up on its landward side, and unfortunately have completely destroyed its original context (*28*).

Although it is boarded up and currently unused, it retains some of its original surface rendering and is in a reasonable condition. Internally there is no enclosed magazine area, but it is possible that the internal brickwork was removed at some stage in the past. The tower apparently still retains its original gun carriage, although the gun itself was dismounted in 1940. The sea wall of the Tower has been knocked through in the past to allow the installation of winching equipment for local fishermen to beach their boats, although this has now been blocked up.

Some 12 concrete anti-tank cubes dating from the Second World War were collected from the surrounding area during the Sovereign Harbour development and deposited around the base of the Tower. Some of these cubes are variations on the local 'standard' anti-tank cube, having either circular or very shallow roots.

28 Martello Tower 64, The Crumbles: housing has recently encroached upon this Martello Tower. The Second World War modifications can be seen on the roof and the blocked-up window, whilst a number of anti-tank cubes lie on the beach around it

Directions and access

To find the Tower, turn off the A259 into Sovereign Harbour (North). At the first roundabout turn left into Pacific Drive. Follow this through the next two roundabouts, and then turn left into Caroline Way, turning left and parking in front of the houses. There is then a short footpath onto the beach, with the Tower in front of you.

The Tower can be visited at any time.

References/Background reading

www.martello-towers.co.uk

SITE 17: PEVENSEY BAY

Period: **Napoleonic to Cold War**
Type of site: **Martello Towers and coastal defences**

History

There are three surviving Martello Towers at Pevensey Bay from the six originally constructed here between 1805 and 1808 (*2*). They were built to cover the low shingle beach that stretched along this part of the south coast, which would have made an ideal landing place for invading French troops.

29 Martello Tower 60, Pevensey Bay: one of three surviving towers at Pevensey Bay, it was turned into a private residence in the early 1980s when a new structure was added to the roof

Martello Tower 60 (*29*) was built on a stone plinth, perhaps to provide better stability, and there is some doubt as to whether the brickwork was originally rendered. The tower was occupied by the Coastguard in the 1840s and was used by the Cinque Ports Artillery Volunteers in 1886. There is no evidence that it was used or modified during the Second World War, possibly due to its current location set back some 250m from the shoreline. The Tower was derelict until 1959, when it was used as a ROC observation post, and it was during this time that the brick staircase to the first floor door on the north side was added.

Martello Tower 61 also stands on a stone plinth, which can clearly be seen at the base of the Tower. Above the plinth there are between four and six courses of yellow bricks showing in the exposed brickwork, whilst the remainder of the Tower appears to have been built from red bricks (*colour plate 9*). A number of brickworks sprang up between Eastbourne and Winchelsea to produce bricks specifically for the construction of the Martello Towers. One such brickfield was located to the east of the Castle Inn (TQ657041) at Pevensey. Although most of these brickworks produced red bricks, yellow bricks were being produced at a brickfield near to Pevensey and Westham railway station later in the nieteenth century. There is evidence that some of the yellow bricks were brought from London to supplement those produced locally.

Nothing is known about the earlier history of Tower 61, but in the 1930s it was being used as a shingle grader. In 1940 a concrete roof was added and a two-storey structure placed on top of it. This structure contained range-finding equipment for the adjacent Emergency Coastal Battery. After the war the Tower was converted into a residence with additional windows, an extra door and a metal stairway, which provided access to the first floor.

Martello Tower 62 was built from a random mix of red and yellow bricks. It was used as a Coast Guard station in the 1830s and was still manned by Coastguards in 1851. It was used as a residence before the Second World War, and photographic evidence shows a windowed structure had been added to the roof and a new door at ground level. During the Second World War the Tower was requisitioned and the roof structure was reinforced with concrete. Following the war the Tower remained derelict for a while but was then renovated, with some windows and a flat-roofed brick-built ground floor extension being added on the west side, and it was once again used as a residence.

Of the other Martello Towers at Pevensey Bay, Tower 59 at TQ662043 was sited to defend the Pevensey Haven sluices and was later used by the Coastguard. It was demolished in 1903 to make way for housing development. Tower 63, which was located to the west of Tower 62 at TQ649027, was probably demolished just prior to the Second World War.

During the Second World War, the stretch of coastline from Pevensey Bay to Eastbourne had two rows of anti-tank cubes, with scaffolding at the top of the beach and 15ft high scaffolding on the sands. A map drawn up by 5th Battalion, The Kings Regiment, covering the battalion area between the Crumbles and Normans' Bay shows the double row of anti-tank cubes, numerous minefields and the location of individual weapon pits.

An Emergency Coastal Battery of two ex-naval 5.5in BL Mk I guns was positioned on the beach to the east of Martello Tower 61 in May 1941 and manned by 237 Coast Battery, which had been formed on 7 March 1941. The battery was located at The Pink House with the two guns mounted on the beach, one on each side of the property. Two 90cm searchlights were provided, No.1 being 113yds to the west of No.1 Gun and the No.2 searchlight 146yds east of No.2 Gun. Three spigot mortars were provided for local defence and in May 1943 two 40mm Bofors guns were added for air defence. According to battery standing orders dated 10 July 1942, No. 1 Gun was controlled by the battery observation post situated in Martello Tower 61 and No. 2 Gun was controlled by a section observation post. The offices were accommodated in The Pink House, whilst the remainder of the personnel were billeted in four cottages in The Beachings. The Home Guard apparently manned two ex-US 75mm field guns as flank protection for the battery.

The sites today

Tower 60 was turned into a private residence in the early 1980s, when new windows were added and a structure placed on the roof. Tower 61 is now surrounded by a housing estate built in the 1960s with the Tower as its focal point. The Second World War structure has been retained as part of the residence, but it is not known whether it is occupied at present. Martello Tower 62, which is known as the 'Grey Tower', is located in a caravan park of the same name and is currently used as a residence.

Very little survives of the Second World War Emergency Coastal Battery. A concrete base and the low concrete front wall are all that remains of a gun position on the east side of the The Beachings, formerly The Pink House (TQ 6548 0355). Within the walls of this property, and to the rear of the gun position, is a small rectangular building with a thick concrete roof that may have been associated with the battery, perhaps an engine room.

Photographic evidence shows that almost all of the beach defences had been removed by 1946, and the beach was once again being used for recreational activities. However, in The Beachings (TQ 6545 0361), there are eight anti-tank buoys lining the south side of the road, whilst another four are located at the south end of Val Prinseps Road (TQ 6550 0365). There are also two very eroded anti-tank cubes on the beach outside the Grey Tower Caravan Park.

Along the Coast Road towards Normans' Bay are 16 anti-tank pimples, which have been repositioned to line the grass verge between the road and a dyke (TQ 6685 0475). Closer to Pevensey Bay in an Environment Agency depot astride the Coast Road, five Nissen huts are located (TQ 6616 0438); three on the north side of the road and two on the south side.

Directions and access

Tower 60 is located in a housing estate at TQ 6556 0389. It can be reached by turning off the A259 into Leyland Road next to the car showrooms and is then immediately on the right-hand side. There is no access to the Tower as it is a private residence, but it can be viewed from the road.

Tower 61 is located in Millward Road in the Martello Estate at TQ 6528 0350. It can be reached by turning off the A259 into the housing estate on the western side of Pevensey Bay. Although the Tower is a private residence it can be approached and viewed from the road or adjacent paved area.

Tower 62 is located in the Grey Tower Caravan Park at TQ 6509 0307, which is off the A259 to the west of Pevensey Bay. But as the Tower is on private property, it is best viewed by walking along the beach from Tower 61.

The Emergency Coastal Battery position is reached by turning off the A259 down Val Princeps Road. Park here and walk onto the beach towards the large villa complex that was formerly The Pink House. The anti-tank buoys can be found along The Beachings, which is a private road.

The Coast Road runs east from the centre of Pevensey Bay to Normans' Bay (see Site 20); the pimples are situated on the left side of the road at the junction with Marine Parade.

References/Background reading
Brook, D. 1992, *Pevensey, Westham and District: A Portrait in Old Picture Postcards*, Seaford, S.B. Publications

PRO WO 192/75

www.martello-towers.co.uk

SITE 18: PEVENSEY CASTLE

Period: **Tudor and Second World War**
Type of site: **Gun emplacement, command post and pillboxes**

History

At the end of the third century AD a fort was constructed on the peninsula of high ground that projected from the mainland into Pevensey Bay. This fort, covering an area of 4ha, was one of at least 10 'Shore Forts' built around the south-east and East Anglian coastline at this time, and its position protected a possible harbour to its north and provided a base for the Roman army protecting the coastline. After 1066, the ruined defences were taken over by the Norman invaders and in the centuries that followed the keep and inner bailey were constructed in the eastern corner of the Roman fort.

A survey of 1573 records that the castle buildings were ruinous, but the threat of the Spanish Armada led to the construction of a gun emplacement in the south-east of the Roman fort. This M-shaped earthwork comprises a slightly raised platform some 20m in size, with a low bank on its seaward side, and was armed with two 'Demi-culverins of small value'. This gun emplacement, together with those at Rockhouse Bank and to the rear of Pevensey Bay (see Site 20), was designed to cover the entrance to Pevensey Harbour.

In 1940 the castle was used as a command post and was garrisoned by Canadian and British troops. Established as a key defence point, the castle was refortified with a number of pillboxes and machine gun posts, which were constructed under the supervision of the Ministry of Works. The gates of the Roman fort were closed by the addition of concrete walls, as were the gates of the medieval Inner Bailey. A total of 48 anti-tank cubes were positioned along the fallen south wall, whilst further cubes and obstacles blocked a gap in the north wall and were positioned near the Roman gates. In addition, roadblocks, anti-tank obstacles and pillboxes covered the roads into Pevensey from the east and from Pevensey Bay, and into Westham from the south and west. No. 17 Bridge End (now demolished) was requisitioned and a machine gun emplaced there covering Pevensey Bridge. Later in the war the castle was taken over by the Home Guard and in 1944 it was used by the US Army Air Corps.

The following installations were constructed at Pevensey Castle, using brick and concrete faced with flint and occasionally sandstone rubble, in such a way as to both assist the camouflaging of the positions and not detract from the character of the historic monument (*30*):

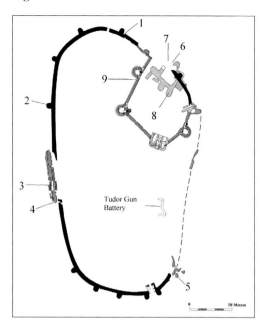

30 Plan of Pevensey Castle showing the location of the Second World War defences

1. A square pillbox was added to the wall on the south-east side of the East Gate adjacent to the Roman bastion (TQ 6454 0484). It has an embrasure facing east over the wall. Its original entrance can be seen on its south side within the Roman fort.

2. A square pillbox built into a Roman bastion on the north-west wall (TQ 6444 0489) with a single embrasure facing north-west across Castle Road and an entrance in its rear side.

3. A square free-standing pillbox built amongst the collapsed Roman fort wall on the north-west side (TQ 6437 0484). It sits on a concrete base, with a single embrasure facing north-west across Castle Road.

4. A square pillbox built into the collapsed Roman fort wall on the north-west side adjacent to the postern gate (TQ 6436 0483) with a single embrasure facing south-west along Castle Road.

5. A machine gun emplacement built into the collapsed Roman wall in the south corner of the fort (TQ 6436 0467). This position has two embrasures, facing south-west and south-east respectively (*31*).

6. A square pillbox built against the eastern buttress of the keep (TQ 6456 0479) with a single embrasure facing east. This pillbox also has concrete steps leading to an access in its north wall.

31 Pevensey Castle: machine gun emplacement (No. 5) built into the collapsed Roman wall in the south corner of the fort. The two embrasures face south-west and south-east

7. Positioned below and just to the north of Pillbox 6 is a sub-rectangular machine gun emplacement, built into the collapse of the keep (*32*). This emplacement has three embrasures, two side-by-side facing east and the third facing south-east.

8. An observation post and machine gun emplacement incorporated into the highest surviving part of the keep (TQ 6454 0477). This has two embrasures, one facing south (*colour plate 10*) and the second facing north-east.

9. A machine gun emplacement has been inserted into the north wall of the medieval castle. It is located on the west side of the East Tower, and was accessed (blocked by a grille today) from the entrance to the East Tower inside the castle. The interior of the emplacement has been reinforced with brick and concrete. The embrasure is also blocked, but can been seen from the north part of the Roman Fort.

10. An anti-tank blockhouse was built in the mouth of the Roman West Gate, but was removed at the end of the war.

11. Two pillboxes of an unknown type were built to the east of the medieval keep, in the area that is now the car park. These were removed after the war and no trace of them survives today.

32 Pevensey Castle: a square pillbox (No. 6) built into the eastern buttress of the keep can be seen on the left, with a machine gun emplacement (No. 7) built into the collapse of the keep on its lower right

12. A position for a 2pdr anti-tank gun was prepared within the Roman fort between the path and the north wall. It is not clear whether this was ever occupied and no trace of it survives today, although a recent geophysical survey shows an anomaly at its supposed location.

Other changes were made to Pevensey Castle during the war to enable it to be used as a command post and barracks. These included the lining of the interior of the medieval towers with bricks, the insertion of wooden floors and glazed windows, and the installation of concrete roofs.

Although many people from Pevensey were evacuated or chose to leave, two surface air-raid shelters were built at Pevensey Primary School to provide shelter for those who remained and for the soldiers stationed in the hutted camp south of Vicarage Cottage and the Village Hall. Anti-aircraft guns were positioned on Pevensey Common and south of Pevensey Bay railway station.

The site today
Pevensey Castle today is an outstanding example of a location that has been of strategic importance for almost 2000 years. The continuity shown by its Roman, medieval, Tudor and Second World War defences on one hand provides examples of how warfare has changed, but on the other demonstrates the importance of the need to dominate an important piece of ground.

At the end of the war, most of the military installations were left in situ except for the anti-tank blockhouse (No. 10) and the pillboxes outside the castle (No. 11), which were removed. All of the pillboxes and emplacements have had their entrances and embrasures blocked up, but can be viewed from the outside. Pillboxes 6-9 can only be accessed through the medieval castle, although they can also be seen from the castle car park.

The Tudor gun emplacement can also be seen in the south-eastern part of the Roman fort, and is marked with a plaque. A recent geophysical survey has shown that this emplacement did not seem to be protected by a ditch or any other earthworks. A cannon found within the fort may have originally been positioned in this emplacement. The cannon was cast in Sussex and is marked with a Tudor Rose and the initials E.R. It is currently mounted on a replica carriage in the Inner Bailey of the medieval castle.

Only one of the surface air-raid shelters in Pevensey now survives, the other having been demolished to make way for the new Fire Station. The remaining shelter is of standard brick construction with a concrete roof (TQ 6484 0492). Its original entrance has been blocked with breezeblocks and a new larger doorway inserted in one wall.

Directions and access

To find Pevensey Castle, take the B2191 into Pevensey from the roundabout on the A27. The castle is in front of you on a sharp left-hand bend, but turn right past the pub and into the castle car park. Park here and walk back to the Roman East Gate.

The air-raid shelter is situated at the rear of the Fire Station and Pevensey Memorial Hall in Church Lane. Note the single anti-tank buoy at the front of the Memorial Hall.

Pevensey Castle can also be reached by train. Alight at Pevensey Bay station, which is half a mile from the castle.

There is also a small local Museum in Pevensey High Street.

Opening times
The exterior and interior of the Roman fort can be accessed at any time, but the medieval castle is in the ownership of English Heritage and there is a charge for entry.

1 April–30 September, daily 10.00am–6.00pm.
1–31 October, daily 10.00am–4.00pm.
1 November–31 March, Saturday and Sunday only 10.00am–4.00pm.

References/Background reading
Butler, C. 2005, *A Geophysical Survey of Pevensey Castle, East Sussex*, Unpublished MSFAT Report

Foot, W. 2006, *Beaches, fields, streets and hills: the anti-invasion landscapes of England*, CBA Research Report 144, York, Council for British Archaeology

Gibbs, L. 2003, *Pevensey Castle Conservation Statement*, London, English Heritage

Goodall, J. 1999, *Pevensey Castle*, London, English Heritage

Ockenden, M. 2006, *Canucks by the Sea*, Eastbourne, CPI Antony Rowe

Pearson, A. 2002, *The Roman Shore Forts*, Stroud, Tempus Publishing Ltd

SITE 19: WESTHAM AND STONE CROSS

Period: **Nineteenth century to Second World War**
Type of site: **Drill hall and observation post**

History

The Drill Hall located at TQ 6382 0439 was built around 1892. It comprised a large open hall at ground floor level, with offices and other rooms on the first floor. During the First World War it was used for training. At the start of the Second World War the Drill Hall was used as a reception centre for children evacuated from London. One evacuee described her journey and subsequent stay in Westham, including visits to both Pevensey Castle and the beach at Pevensey Bay in September 1939. Other than this the Drill Hall does not appear to have been used during the war.

In 1940 a roadblock, comprising 'hairpin' rails, covered by two pillboxes, was located across the Eastbourne Road to the south of the railway crossing and anti-tank blocks surrounded the road junction with the Stone Cross road, where another road block and pillbox were situated. These were part of the outer defences for Pevensey Castle (see Site 18); however by 1941 only the roadblock on the Pevensey to Stone Cross road and two machine gun positions south of the railway line are shown on the Battalion Area Map of 5th Battalion The Kings Regiment.

The Windmill at Stone Cross (TQ6195 0428) is a brick-built tower mill, built in 1875/6. It ceased working commercially in 1937 and during the Second World War was taken over by the Canadian Army and used as an observation post by 28th Battery of 5th Canadian Field Regiment in 1940. The west side of the windmill roundel was reinforced with a concrete roof and a machine gun was mounted on it.

Located close to the windmill was a pillbox covering the road (B2247) from Stone Cross to Westham, as well as the railway line running across Mountney Level.

The sites today

The Drill Hall is now used for light industrial and commercial purposes, but can be viewed from outside (*33*). There is no surviving evidence for the roadblocks or pillboxes at Westham, although some of the rail sockets survived until recently.

33 Drill Hall, Westham: built around 1892 for the local volunteers and later used by the Territorial Army. Now used for light industrial and commercial purposes

After the war Stone Cross windmill remained derelict until the 1960s, having been designated a Grade II★ Listed Building in 1952. Restoration by the Stone Cross Mill Trust to its 1880 condition started in 1998 and was completed in 2000. The reinforced concrete roof added to the roundel was removed during the restoration, but on the first floor adjacent to the door onto the roundel roof, some graffiti left by Canadian soldiers has been retained.

The pillbox covering the B2247 is still extant at TQ 6216 0435. It is of concrete construction with a chamfered roof edge and appears to have embrasures on its east and south sides. An internal division forms a blast wall inside the entrance, which is on the north-west corner. The pillbox is very overgrown and it was not possible to get inside or fully survey it on a field visit in 2006.

Directions and access

The Drill Hall is located on the north side of the level crossing adjacent to Pevensey and Westham railway station, on the B2191 (Eastbourne Road). Limited parking may be possible in Montague Way opposite the Drill Hall.

Stone Cross Windmill is open each Sunday between 2-5pm from April to September. Access is from Beggars Lane, which can be found by taking Rattle Road (B2247) from Westham to Stone Cross. There is no parking at the Windmill, but cars can be parked in a layby on the B2247, or adjacent roads. There is no access to the pillbox, which is on private land.

References/Background reading

Donaldson, B, 2005 www.bbc.co.uk/ww2peopleswar/stories/20/a4627820.
shtml

Foot, W. 2006, *Beaches, fields, streets and hills: the anti-invasion landscapes of England*,
CBA Research Report 144, York, Council for British Archaeology

Stone Cross Windmill Leaflet (undated), Stone Cross Mill Trust

www.sussexmillsgroup.org.uk

SITE 20: NORMANS' BAY

Period: **Tudor to Second World War**
Type of site: **Martello Tower, coastal batteries and anti-tank obstacles**

History

Two batteries were constructed in the sixteenth century to the rear of Normans'
Bay and Pevensey Bay. The first was located at Rockhouse Bank (TQ 6791 0561),
an area of higher ground some 500m inland that dominates the lower ground to
its south. The second battery was located at TQ 6625 0514 on flat lower ground,
presumably covering a now lost inlet. Both of these batteries were recorded in the
survey of 1587 and with the battery at Pevensey Castle would have covered the
entrance to Pevensey Harbour, which due to silting and coastal erosion migrated
eastwards towards Normans' Bay during the sixteenth century. It is possible that
Rockhouse Bank battery was reused during the Napoleonic period. It was used
during the Second World War, when 5th Battalion, The Kings Regiment had a
platoon position with two Bren guns and an anti-tank rifle located there, with an
HQ located in the nearby farmhouse.

Along with the now demolished Tower 54, Martello Tower 55 supported the
battery located at Rockhouse Bank. In 1820 it was fitted with a semaphore
machine, and was used for wireless telegraphy experiments in the early
twentieth century. By 1910 it was used as a summer residence, with extra doors
and windows inserted and a balcony added. In 1940 it was used as an observation
post for the nearby Emergency Coastal Battery and a concrete roof was added
to the Tower.

Construction of an Emergency Coastal Battery at Normans' Bay (TQ 6885
0560) was started on 1 August 1940. Two 4.7in QF MkV★ guns, that had originally
been made for Japanese destroyers in the First World War, but had then been
stored until 1940 in Gibraltar, were mounted in the battery on 21 August 1940.
Two 90cm searchlights were located on the flanks of the battery, with four spigot
mortars and three Vickers machine guns being provided for local protection,
together with a 2in UP (Unrotating Projectile) projector for air defence. The
battery was manned by three officers and 108 other ranks of 375 Coast Battery

RA (part of 552 Coast Regiment RA), which had been formed on 22 July 1940. Existing buildings were requisitioned and some new structures constructed for use by the battery. Defence posts were located on each flank and a pillbox was situated to the rear of the battery, all manned by the infantry, who also occupied further posts on the high ground, some 500yds to the rear.

As with other beaches along the East Sussex coast, the shingle beach at Normans' Bay was heavily defended with anti-tank cubes, barbed wire and mines that were positioned in July 1940. There were probably also pillboxes and other defensive sites, although little evidence of these survives today. Anti-glider posts were erected inland on the flat ground between Pevensey and Bexhill.

The sites today

The Rockhouse Bank battery survives as a three-sided earthwork facing south, and comprising a ditch with an inner rampart some 37.5m in length, with flanking arms each 20m long at its west and east ends. There are no internal features, and two gaps in the rampart and two causeways over the ditch may be later mutilations. Rockhouse Bank battery remains quite an impressive site, with the ditch and bank surviving as significant earthworks, and dominating the lower ground towards the coast.

The second battery is marked by a slight trace of a semi-circular ditch and internal rampart, facing south-east and measuring some 35m overall. The ditch is just about visible in the pasture field, with the rampart hidden by the long grass. A group of 11 anti-tank buoys are situated at TQ 6708 0565 on the edge of the road and in an adjacent field entrance. These are probably not in their original location, but will have come from a nearby roadblock.

Martello Tower 55 (TQ 6807 0530) is looking rather dilapidated today, fenced off and boarded up, with houses and gardens encroaching on its northern side (*colour plate 11*). Located further east at TQ 6980 0612, adjacent to some fishermans' huts is a square concrete block measuring 32in x 32in with a steel pin mounted in its top centre. This is almost certainly a pivot for the cannon mounting from a destroyed Martello Tower. Many of the older houses and other buildings at Normans' Bay have been built from the distinctive yellow bricks reused from destroyed Martello Towers.

The only remains of the Emergency Coastal Battery itself is a concrete base, perhaps part of the War Shelter that was located to the rear of No. 1 Gun. Situated nearby on the north side of the road in a field at TQ 6885 0570 is a semi-sunken concrete bunker with a brick entrance at its north end, possibly originally an ammunition store for the battery. The most impressive remains of the battery complex, however, are the two searchlight posts. No. 1 searchlight was located adjacent to 'Beach Crest' (TQ 6875 0561), a house that had been built in 1939 (using bricks from a demolished Martello Tower), and was then immediately requisitioned by the Army. The searchlight was located in a brick-built two-storey post with removable timber shutters at the front to protect the light when not in use (*colour plate 12*).

A passageway was constructed between the upper storey of the post and the house in which the crew were billeted. An original board retained by the owner of the property after the war gives the following information:

---

552 COAST REGIMENT R.A.
375 COAST BATTERY R.A.
No 1 LAMP Mk III PROJECTOR Mk V
N.O.B. 150°   ARC 100° - 210°
LAMP ATTENDANT i/c :-

No. 2 searchlight was located at 'Beach Cottages' to the east of the battery (TQ 6896 0573), and has been fully incorporated into the house now standing at this location.

A number of anti-tank cubes survive in their original position at the top of the beach, although most were removed immediately after the war (*34*). They were originally erected in a line in front of the pre-war bungalows (which had been requisitioned and were used by the defending troops) and now provide foundation supports for extensions and decking that have been added to the bungalows. Remains of other cubes can be found on the north side of the beach centred on TQ678052, whilst two cubes are situated at Martello Tower 55. Some rusting PSP (Pierced Steel Planking) tracking can also be found on the beach at TQ 6756 0508.

34 Normans' Bay: a number of anti-tank cubes are still in-situ at the top of the beach, in front of the bungalows. Many have been used as foundations for extensions and decking

Directions and access

Rockhouse Bank battery is marked on the Ordnance Survey 1:25000 map and can be reached along the minor road from Normans' Bay to Pevensey, although it is on private property and there are no parking places. The second battery is on the north side of the same road closer to the Pevensey roundabout, but is difficult to see due to erosion as a result of cultivation. The anti-tank buoys can be found on the same road, between the two batteries; they are located on the south side of the road on a sharp corner.

Martello Tower 55 and the other sites at Normans' Bay beach can be reached by taking the Coast Road from Pevensey Bay, past Beachlands. Park in the small layby on the left, just before reaching the caravan park. From here walk onto the beach to see all of the remaining sites mentioned above. The anti-tank cubes incorporated into the bungalows can be found by walking west along the top of the beach between TQ 6748 0499 and TQ 6740 0495, although please remember that these are people's homes.

References/Background reading

Lower, M.A. 1870, *Survey of the Coast of Sussex, made in 1587 — with a view to its defence against Foreign Invasion and especially against the Spanish Armada*, Lewes, W.E. Baxter

East Sussex SMR: TQ60 NE10-MES96; TQ 0 NE6-MES4742

PRO WO 192/74

SITE 21: BEXHILL-ON-SEA

Period: **Napoleonic to the Second World War**
Type of site: **Barracks, drill hall, pillboxes, anti-tank obstacles and air-raid shelter**

History

The first barracks in Bexhill were opened in 1794 when 700 men of the Cheshire Militia were stationed there. In 1804 Bexhill became a depot for the newly formed Kings German Legion (KGL) and by 1805 some 3500 men were housed in wooden huts. The barracks were located near to Old Town in Bexhill, where the road names (Barrack Road and Hanover Close) provide clues to its location. A painting by Francis Grose shows the west end of the barracks having some substantial timber-framed buildings (*3*). As most of the KGL served overseas during the Peninsular campaign, the number of soldiers in the barracks was reduced so that by 1811 it had become an artillery barracks and stores for the KGL. On Napoleon's abdication in 1814, the KGL returned home to Hanover and it is likely that the barracks were dismantled soon afterwards.

Martello Towers 42 to 50 were constructed along the coast from Glyne Gap to Cooden, but none of these survive today. Some fell victim to the eroding coastline soon after their construction, whilst the remaining towers had all disappeared by 1880. Bricks recovered from Tower 42 were used in the building of St Mark's Church in Little Common, Bexhill in 1842, and when this church was extended in 1845, the bricks came from another demolished Martello Tower.

The first Drill Hall in Bexhill was built for a battery of the 1st Cinque Ports Volunteer Artillery in the later nineteenth century and was located between the Queens Head in Belle Hill and London Road. A new Drill Hall was built for the local artillery volunteers in 1901, but was then enlarged in 1914 by a matching additional drill hall on its western side for the Territorial Army (*colour plate 13*). During the First World War a large camp was built at Cooden in 1914 comprising wooden huts and bell tents to house the newly raised volunteer battalions of the Royal Sussex Regiment. These battalions left in 1915, but the camp continued in use until the end of the war.

During the Second World War the beach at Bexhill was defended with barbed wire on the railings along the edge of the promenade and scaffolding and barbed wire on the beach. Minefields were also laid on the beach and anti-tank cubes were placed to block vulnerable landing places. A number of pillboxes were also constructed along the seafront.

Two Emergency Coastal Batteries were also established on the seafront at Bexhill. Both of these were equipped with two ex-naval 6in guns and two 90cm searchlights. The first battery (221 Coast Battery) was situated in the garden of 209 Cooden Drive ('The Bluff') at Cooden Beach, with the two concrete gun positions at the seaward end of the garden (TQ712065). The house was requisitioned for accommodation and its dining room was reinforced to store ammunition, whilst a second ammunition bunker was also constructed in the garden. A pillbox was positioned in the south-west corner of the garden. The second battery was situated on the East Parade at TQ747072 opposite the Sackville Hotel (385 (later 301) Coast Battery). The Royal Artillery originally manned both batteries, but later most of 301 Coast Battery was crewed by the local Home Guard.

Galley Hill was used as an observation post (OP) in 1940. Spike Milligan was stationed in Bexhill after joining 56 Heavy Regiment and described the OP as being 'crude wood heaped with earth' and included a sketch of the OP in his 1972 book. The 56 Heavy Regiment used 9.2in howitzers dating from the First World War to supplement the coastal batteries along the south coast. Milligan also mentions that there were other OP's located in a Martello Tower at Pevensey and at Constables Farm on the Bexhill to Eastbourne road, whilst the Battery headquarters was located at an evacuated girls' school called Worthingholm in Hastings Road, with its telephone exchange in an air-raid shelter at the back of the school.

Anti-aircraft guns (probably Bofors) were located along South Cliff and in Buxton Drive recreation ground, and during Operation Diver a battery of 3.7in guns was positioned on West Parade.

Numerous public air-raid shelters were built across the town, whilst others were located at schools. ARP Warden's Posts were also located around the town, sometimes utilising existing buildings, but also in purpose built structures. The locations of these and other civil defence sites are shown on a map prepared by the Borough engineer and surveyor in 1942 and now held by Bexhill Museum.

The town's Observer Corps post was initially located in a wooden building in the east cupola of The Colonnade, but was then re-sited at Pankhurst Rise, Sidley, and was finally moved to Cooden Golf course in November 1940. After the war an ROC post was set up on Galley Hill in 1949, with an underground concrete bunker being added alongside during the 1950s. It remained operational until 1968 when it was filled in and grassed over.

The sites today

Nothing can be seen today of the extensive KGL encampments at Bexhill. Barrack Road Memorial Gardens mark the location of the barracks burial ground, however, apart from a signboard there is nothing to see. Bexhill Museum has a display on the history of the KGL and their association with the town. There are some military graves dating from this period in the churchyard of the Parish Church of St Peter.

There is also little trace of the Martello Towers. Tower 44 was located on the site of the current Coastguard lookout on Galley Hill, whilst a curved extension of the promenade ('The Horn') in front of the De La Warr Pavilion is probably the site of Tower 46.

The Drill Hall has an interesting crenulated façade, which hides a more modern-looking structure to its rear. The 1914 (western) part of the Drill Hall is still utilised by 14 (Bexhill) Platoon of the Army Cadet Force and 2262 (Bexhill) Squadron of the Air Training Corps, however the original (eastern) side was demolished in 2006.

Of the Second World War remains, some of the anti-tank cubes and the base of a pillbox can be seen east of Galley Hill (see Site 22). In Sidley five anti-tank cylinders forming a wall survive at the Smith & Humphrey Garage (TQ 7391 0926), at the junction of Ninfield Road and All-Saints Lane. These are unlikely to be in their original position, but could indicate the presence of a roadblock nearby. On an S-bend on the A259 (Barnhorn Road), an anti-tank coffin and a cube could be found until recently in the garden of one of the houses (TQ 7062 0787), whilst in Little Common Road there are two anti-tank pimples in the front garden of a house (TQ 7153 0793). These mark the positions of the roadblocks at the west and east ends of a restricted area at Little Common that ran along the ridge between these two points.

Nothing can be seen today of either of the coastal batteries, although one of the gun emplacements of the Cooden Beach battery was retained as a shelter in the garden of The Bluff, together with the ammunition store, until its sale in 1973 when subsequent redevelopment removed them. At Cooden Moat there are a large number of anti-tank cubes dumped into the moat (TQ 7083 0728). These probably originated from the seafront defences.

The OP on Galley Hill appears to have been a temporary construction and there is no evidence of it surviving today. Nearby is a partly buried square concrete pillbox or emplacement (TQ 7599 0775), with only its chamfered roof currently visible after recent landscaping. It appears to be facing east, covering the beach at Glyne Gap, with its view south blocked by Galley Hill.

A surface air-raid shelter survives in Upper Sea Road at TQ 7455 0782 and is built into the embankment on the east side of the road (*35*). Another shelter, of an unusual design, is located opposite the Hospital, at TQ 7441 0855. The shelter at Worthingholme School (now part of Charters Towers in Hastings Road) was relocated by Spike Milligan in 1962, but appears to have been subsequently demolished to make way for housing.

Directions and access

The Barrack Road Memorial Gardens can be found by taking the B2182 (Upper Sea Road) from the railway station; pass under the King Offa Way road and Barrack Road is the first turning on the left. To find the Drill Hall, turn off the A259 into Down Road; the Drill Hall is immediately on the right hand side, with a small car park in front of it.

The first air-raid shelter is located halfway along Upper Sea Road, between the railway station and Old Town. Continue through Old Town towards the Hospital to find the second shelter at the junction of Chantry Avenue with Holliers Hill. Galley Hill is on the seafront at the east end of De La Warr Parade.

Bexhill Museum is located in Egerton Road, and is signposted from the town centre.

35 Bexhill: surviving surface air-raid shelter built into the embankment in Upper Sea Road (TQ 7455 0782)

Cooden Moat can be reached by footpath from Maple Walk.

Opening times
Bexhill Museum is open February to mid-December. Opening times are: Tuesday to Friday 10am-5pm, Saturday and Sunday 2pm-5pm. It is closed on Mondays. There is a small charge for entrance.

The other sites can be visited at any reasonable time.

References/Background reading
Bartley, L.J. 1971, *The Story of Bexhill*, Bexhill-on-Sea, F. J. Parsons Ltd

Bexhill Hanoverian Study Group 2003, *The Kings German Legion*, Bexhill-on-Sea, Bexhill Museum

Burton, D. 1994, *Bexhill's part in the UK Air Attack Warning System 1929-65*, Unpublished note, Bexhill Museum

Chappell, M. 2000, *The Kings German Legion (1) 1803-1812*, Oxford, Osprey Publishing

Lowry, B. (ed.) 1996, *20th Century Defences in Britain: An Introductory Guide*, York, Council for British Archaeology, 67-71

Milligan, S. 1972, *Adolf Hitler – My part in his downfall*, London, Penguin Books

Porter, J. 2004, *Bexhill on Sea, A History*, Chichester, Phillimore

Sussex Express 1985, The War in East Sussex, 2nd ed. Lewes, Sussex Express & County Herald

PRO 116418; WO 44/53

SITE 22: BULVERHYTHE, HASTINGS

Period: **Second World War**
Type of site: **Anti-tank obstacles**

History
The seafront between Bexhill and Hastings would have been an important landing place for German troops during Operation Sealion. This was recognised and the beach was heavily defended with anti-tank cubes, barbed wire and other obstacles, together with a number of pillboxes. A German aerial photograph taken in 1940 clearly shows the two, and sometimes three, lines of anti-tank cubes along Hastings seafront.

In 1944 a troop of four 40mm Bofors anti-aircraft guns were situated at Glyne Gap during Operation Diver and were photographed positioned behind the line of anti-tank cubes on the beach.

The sites today

After the war most of the cubes along the seafront at Hastings and Bexhill were removed, but at Bulverhythe, between the two towns, there are still many in evidence. The surviving cubes are 5ft 4in tall divided into two equal halves; the lower half (the root), would be buried in the ground, whilst the upper exposed half is 3ft 8in square and has a 12in high pyramidal addition on the top. Starting at the west end, near Galley Hill in Bexhill, and stretching along the beach to the West Marina in Hastings, the following sites were recorded in 2006:

1. At the east end of this beach (TQ 7648 0791) are three in situ anti-tank cubes adjacent to the low cliff and beside a row of beach huts. These examples are in good condition (*36*).

2. Twenty metres to the east of these cubes, on the cliff edge (TQ 7650 0792), is the concrete base of a Type 24 pillbox. This pillbox has been demolished, but the bottom of its concrete walling retained between brick shuttering can still be seen. Coastal erosion is undermining the concrete base.

3. Located at the rear of some beach huts at TQ 7693 0814 is a single cube, probably in its original position.

4. Scattered on the beach at TQ 7737 0833 are the shattered remains of some 30 concrete cubes. Recent construction of anti-erosion beach defences here may have buried or destroyed other examples.

36 Bulverhythe: three in-situ anti-tank cubes on the beach at TQ 7648 0791, with the base of a demolished pillbox eroding from the cliff at top right

5. A group of eight surviving cubes are located at TQ 7779 0853. Five in reasonable condition survive in one line side by side, approximately 1m apart. Thirty metres further east are an additional three cubes. All of these appear to be in their original position.

6. A single uprooted cube is located at TQ 7812 0863. This has been reused to block a path behind some beach huts.

7. Two cubes, also uprooted, have been reused to block a gap onto the beach between two groups of beach huts at TQ 7842 0864. These are in good condition and clearly show the root of the cube, normally buried below ground.

8. The final two remaining cubes are located at the West Marina in Hastings (TQ 7851 0867). These are probably in their original location, set at an oblique angle to the beach frontage to cover the metalled access onto the beach.

Also located on the beach at Bulverhythe is the Protected Historic Wreck of the *Amsterdam*. This ship was run aground here in 1749 and its outline can be seen in the sand at extremely low tides. More information on the *Amsterdam* can be found in the Hasting Shipwreck Heritage Centre.

Directions and access

Park at Galley Hill at the east end of Bexhill seafront and walk east along the coast. The central part, and the *Amsterdam*, can also be accessed from Bridge Way off the A259. Alternatively, there is a car park at the West Marina, Hastings. To find this, turn off the A259 into Cinque Ports Way, go past the Territorial Army centre and turn left into the car park.

References/Background reading

Defence of Britain project: 1940/10/23 Taktisches Luftbildbuch Nr. 3

SITE 23: HASTINGS

Period: **Tudor to Second World War**
Type of site: **Town wall, batteries and anti-tank obstacles**

History

Hastings was one of the Cinque Ports, providing England with ships and men for its defence since at least 1155 in return for special privileges. A defensive wall stood at the southern end of Hastings Old Town by the middle of the sixteenth century. There were three gates (the Seagates) through the wall and two forts or batteries; one at the western end of the wall (at the west end of George Street) and one at the eastern end of the wall on the seafront. The forts are shown on a map of 1746 and were there prior to 1610. In 1626/7 they received four Demi-culverins and two Sakers, but by 1656 only two guns were mounted. In 1690 after the naval engagement off Beachy Head, the town's guns fired at French ships, which in return fired into the town.

The town wall was redundant by the mid eighteenth century and was being robbed for building material. In 1759 a new battery was built to the west of the original west fort and it later mounted some eleven 12pdr guns. It was demolished in 1832 after being damaged in the storms of 1824. The original east fort may have been rebuilt in 1759, as by 1831 it mounted six 24pr guns. The building of the harbour arm in 1896 and the groyne at Rock-a-Nore in 1887 completely changed the area of The Stade, as shingle built up to form the current seafront.

The shingle beach at Hastings would have been one of the landing places for the German army during Operation Sealion. To counter this, anti-tank cubes and anti-tank pimples were laid along the top of the beach and were backed up by a number of pillboxes. In addition three large Martello Tower-style camouflaged concrete vats were stationed along the seafront at White Rock Gardens, the Fishmarket and Rock-a-Nore. These held oil, which was to be pumped down steel pipes into the sea and set on fire in the event of an invasion (Sea Flame Barrage). Both St Leonards Pier and Hastings Pier had sections removed to ensure that they could not be used by German landing barges.

Although there is little trace of these defences today, an aerial photograph taken by the Luftwaffe in 1940 shows a single line of cubes between the Boating Lake and the beach. This increases to a double line of cubes further east and then a triple line of cubes at The Stade, before reducing back to two lines. The same photograph also shows five pillboxes in the same area, with a further two on the cliffs above.

Hastings was also defended by an Emergency Coastal Battery, which was located at TQ829095 in the area of Rock-a-Nore. This was manned by 360 Coast Battery (552 Coast Regiment) and comprised two 6in MkII guns, the positions for which can also be seen on the Luftwaffe aerial photograph. A flank battery comprising a single 4in Mk9 gun and a single 60pdr MkII gun was located at TQ820094.

There were also a number of anti-aircraft batteries at Hastings. Two Bofors 40mm anti-aircraft guns were located on East Hill (TQ830097), with others on West Hill (TQ824099), in Broomgrove Road near Ore Station (approximately TQ827106) and within pre-cast concrete-block emplacements in Sea Road. In 1944 during Operation Diver a heavy anti-aircraft battery, equipped with seven 3.7in anti-aircraft guns, was located in Sea Road (TQ789087) to counter the V1 threat, whilst another (481 HAA Battery) was situated on West Hill with its command post in the ladies public lavatories at the top of the Cliff Railway.

Public air-raid shelters were provided around the town, whilst many shelters were also constructed at schools. The Grammar School had a number of trenches covered with railway sleepers and sandbags at the entrance. St Clements Caves were also used as an air-raid shelter from October 1940, with an additional entrance opened up in Croft Road. However, the caves were not popular as they were dank, damp and smelly. The ARP headquarters was located in Queens Road, and First Aid Posts were set up at five locations across the town.

The sites today

Little remains today of the Second World War defences on Hastings seafront, with the concrete vats being decommissioned and removed in June 1945. The gun positions of the Emergency Coastal Battery are beneath the Rock-a-Nore car park and the pillboxes all appear to have been demolished. However, there are surviving elements of the defences still to be seen on The Stade and at the east end of Rock-a-Nore Road:

1. A single anti-tank cube is still in its original position between the fishermen's net shops and the beach at TQ 8271 0947.

2. Remains of numerous other cubes can be seen on the beach at TQ 8291 0952, opposite the Hastings Motor Boat and Yacht Club at the east end of Rock-a-Nore Road (*colour plate 14*).

3. At the east end of the Hastings Motor Boat and Yacht Club car park at the end of Rock-a-Nore Road are three anti-tank pimples (TQ 8304 0955). These are in reasonably good condition and appear to be in their original location (*37*).

Although there is no surviving evidence for the anti-aircraft gun positions on West Hill, the public lavatories used as the battery command post still exist at the top of the Cliff Railway (TQ 8218 0959).

Two surface air-raid shelters survive in Old London Road. The first is at High Bank (TQ 8322 1096). It was built into the bank on the east side of the road and is constructed of brick, with a concrete roof and a concrete blast wall protecting the single entrance (now blocked) at the south end (*38*). An emergency exit was also provided at ground level near the north end and comprises a square of weakly bonded bricks below a concrete lintel. An interesting feature is the line of slate edging incorporated into the base of the roof along the side wall. The second shelter is located at the junction with Robertson's Hill (TQ 8289 1055), and is built into the slope on the west side of the road. It has a small entrance annex (now blocked) at one end. Further south along Old London Road, a large air-raid shelter was constructed below the allotments on the west side of the road; its blocked entrance can be seen from the pavement at TQ 8283 1011. Another surviving surface shelter is situated at the entrance to White Rock Gardens (TQ 8113 0934). St Clements Caves (TQ 8235 0986) are open to the public.

Directions and access

From the centre of Hastings turn into Rock-a-Nore Road and continue past the fishermen's net shops on The Stade before turning right into Rock-a-Nore car park (pay and display). From here all the seafront sites are within easy walking distance.

37 Anti-tank pimples at the Hastings Motor Boat and Yacht Club car park at the end of Rock-a-Nore Road, Hastings (TQ 8304 0955)

38 Surface air-raid shelter built into the roadside bank at High Bank, Old London Road, Hastings (TQ 8322 1096)

The Hastings Shipwreck Heritage Centre is located in Rock-a-Nore Road, and has information on the *Amsterdam* wreck (see Site 22) and other local shipwrecks.

The air-raid shelters in Old London Road (A259) can be found by heading north out of Hastings town centre towards Rye. The first is located on the left side of the road at the junction with Robertson's Hill, whilst the second is on the right side of the road just after Mount Road and opposite High Bank; parking on this busy road is difficult. The entrance to the underground shelter below the allotments is situated on the west side of Old London Road opposite the speed camera. The shelter at the entrance to White Rock Gardens can be found off Bohemia Road.

The entrance to St Clements Caves is on the east side of West Hill.

Opening times
The sites can be visited at any reasonable time.

Hastings Shipwreck Heritage Centre: 01424 437452

Opening hours:
    Daily Easter to October : 10.30am–5.00pm
    Daily October to Easter : 11.00am–4.00pm

St Clements Caves: 01424 422964

References/Background reading
Goodwin, N.D. 2005, *Hastings at War 1939-1945*, Chichester, Phillimore
Longstaff-Tyrrell, P. 2002, *Barracks to Bunkers*, Stroud, Sutton Publishing Ltd
Manwaring Baines, J. 1986, *Historic Hastings*, St Leonards-on-Sea, Cinque Ports
    Press Ltd
Porter, M.H. 2002, *Hastings in Peace and War 1930-1945*, Bexhill, Ferndale Press
Defence of Britain Project: 1940/10/23 Taktisches Luftbildbuch Nr. 3

East Sussex SMR: ES7188-MES7188; TQ 80 NW75-MES993

SITE 24: FAIRLIGHT

Period: **Napoleonic to the Cold War**
Type of site: **Signals posts, radar stations and ROC post**

History
An Admiralty Signal Post was opened in 1795 on the 'Firehills' at Fairlight and was later supplemented by a fire beacon. The accommodation hut attached to

1 Camber Castle: Tudor artillery fort initially built 1512-14 and later strengthened by Henry VIII. Now cut off from the coast and lying some way inland

2 The Caponier at Newhaven Fort: entered by a tunnel descending from the interior of the fort, this caponier protected the rear of the Town Battery and the base of the cliffs

3 Newhaven Fort: this 12pdr QF gun with its overhead cover was manned by 101 Coast Battery during the Second World War

4 Tide Mills: a loophole cut through one of the flint walls and facing across the lagoon

5 A Type 25 pillbox looks out across the golf course towards Seaford Head

6 View looking west across Cuckmere Haven. In the foreground is the Type 23 pillbox and in front of this is the surviving stretch of anti-tank ditch

7 Cuckmere Haven: the row of 20 anti-tank cubes set against an earthen bank at TV 5164 9784. The furthest cube has '133 COY, 3 SECT' inscribed into the cement on its top

8 The guardhouse of the First World War St Anthony's airfield at Eastbourne, now used as a bungalow

9 Martello Tower 61, Pevensey Bay: this tower stands on a stone plinth, above which there are a few courses of yellow bricks. The remainder of the Tower has then been built from red bricks

10 Pevensey Castle: an observation post and machine gun emplacement (No. 8) incorporated into the highest surviving part of the medieval Keep

11 Martello Tower 55, Normans' Bay: looking rather dilapidated, but retaining much of its rendering and the concrete roof structure added during the Second World War

12 Normans' Bay ECB, No. 1 searchlight: the searchlight was located in the brick two-storey post on the left. A passageway connected the post and 'Beach Crest' where the crew were billeted

13 Bexhill: the Drill Hall on the right was built for the local artillery volunteers in 1901, and then enlarged in 1914 by the matching building on its left side. Since this picture was taken in early 2006, the original drill hall has been demolished

14 Hastings: uprooted and discarded anti-tank cubes on the beach opposite the Hastings Motor Boat and Yacht Club at the east end of Rock-a-Nore Road

15 Emergency Coastal Battery on Toot Rock, Pett Level: in the foreground is a holdfast for a weapon or searchlight and behind it is the battery observation post

16 Rye Harbour: machine gun emplacement on the shingle beach (TQ 9485 1797)

17 The Brooks, Lewes: a 'squashed' Type 24 pillbox on Lower Rise, situated on the eastern slope and facing east with a superb field of fire towards the River Ouse and Beddingham (TQ 4250 0790)

18 Rodmell: this Type 24 pillbox has been incorporated into a wall around a sports field and is now used as a store and cricket screen (TQ 4223 0633)

19 Barcombe Mills: in the foreground is a Type 24 pillbox (A253), with the Type 28 anti-tank pillbox (A252) a short distance behind. These were positioned on one of the islands covering the easternmost bridges

20 Howbourne Farm, Buxted: pillbox A175 still retains its original camouflage. It is a standard Type 24 pillbox, but has a pitched roof to make it look like a small building (TQ 5128 2506)

21 Old Lodge Warren, Crowborough: a Type 24 pillbox (A110) covers a footbridge across the stream close to a disused pumping station at TQ 5473 3136 and is being badly undermined by erosion

22 Ringmer: this single-storey tiled building may have been the hospital for the Napoleonic artillery barracks

23 Horsebridge, near Hailsham: an unusual machine gun emplacement covers the A22 road bridge over the river Cuckmere (TQ 5747 1106)

24 Bodiam: this Type 28A pillbox sits on a concrete base set into the bank of the Tilt-yard at Bodiam Castle, which can be seen behind it. Note the unusual angled wall on the right side

25 Cripp's Corner: this line of anti-tank cubes to the south of Cripp's Corner stretches from Thorp's Wood and follows field boundaries to the B2244 road

the latter was described in 1806 as being 'built of turf in a ruinous state'. In 1803 the Army established the military telegraph line along the south coast with a post at Fairlight and after the Napoleonic Wars the Admiralty installed a semaphore station, which was 'ready to operate' in 1820.

In 1940 a Chain Home Low (CHL) radar station (RAF Fairlight) was set up on the north side of the Fairlight Road with its two component sites at TQ845117 and TQ849117. During the Operation Diver campaign it was updated to a GCI station, with enhanced radar capability, and was surrounded by anti-aircraft guns. The associated domestic site was located a little further east along the Fairlight Road. There was also a second site at Fairlight called RAF Grangewood. This was operational between 1943 and 1944, and was situated to the east of Fairlight Church along Mill Road (approximately TQ863119). It apparently had two 90ft aerials and a number of Nissen huts, and was associated with a navigational aid system (Type 100 GH) that enabled allied bombers operating over Europe to bomb blind.

In the early 1950s a ROTOR single level R2 bunker and associated radar was set up closer to the coast, and by 1952 had replaced the CHL site, although the domestic site was retained. By 1956 the ROTOR station was redundant and had been placed on a care and maintenance basis until it was finally closed in the early 1960s.

An ROC underground monitoring post was constructed adjacent to the Coastguard lookout tower at Fairlight (TQ 8614 1121). It was opened in 1960 and finally closed in 1991. The ROC personnel also used the lower floor of the adjacent Coastguard lookout.

The sites today

There is no surviving evidence for the CHL site, which was returned to agriculture in the 1950s. Some concrete bases for buildings of the domestic site, together with the service road, survive at TQ849117.

Although the ROTOR bunker was considered as the site for the Hastings Area Civil Defence Control, nothing came of this and the bunker was finally sealed up and all buildings on the site demolished in 1973. The site of the ROTOR bunker can be identified by the large rectangular raised mound near the cliff edge (TQ 8621 1127), with the site of the now demolished guardhouse at its west end (TQ 8615 1125).

Although the ROC post has been closed and locked up, the above ground features all survive within the fenced radar compound in front of the Coastguard lookout (*39*).

In an old quarry to the west of Coastguard Lane, there is a surface air-raid shelter dating to the Second World War (TQ 8578 1145). It is built against the bank of the quarry, and has an entrance and blast wall at the east end, with a separate blast wall and a low entrance at the west end.

39 The above-ground features of the ROC underground monitoring post adjacent to the coastguard lookout tower at Fairlight (TQ 8614 1121)

Directions and access

All the sites at Fairlight are within Hastings Country Park. There are car parks and a visitor centre at the Country Park, which is signposted off the Fairlight Road. To find the ROTOR bunker and ROC post, walk south from the car parks, past the row of cottages to the radar and Coastguard lookout. The air-raid shelter can be found by returning to the cottages and taking the footpath beside them heading west for about 250m; the quarry is on your right.

The domestic site is located alongside the Fairlight Road Picnic Site and car park, which can be found by heading along Fairlight Road towards Hastings from the main entrance to the Country Park.

Access at any reasonable time.

Countryside Ranger: 01424 813225

References/Background reading

Goodwin, J.E. 2000, *Military Signals from the South Coast*, Midhurst, Middleton Press

Haigh, Brig. J.D. 1960, *The Services Textbook of Radio, Volume 7, Radiolocation Techniques*, London, H.M.S.O

www.subbrit.org.uk/rsg/sites/f/fairlight/index.html

SITE 25: PETT LEVEL

Period: Seventeenth century to Second World War
Type of site: Emergency coastal battery and anti-tank obstacles

History

After the Battle of Beachy Head in 1690 (see Site 13), the *Anne* was beached here on 3 July. The *Anne* was the only English ship lost in the battle, and after being heavily damaged was towed eastwards by the *York*. The *Anne* was beached at high tide and it was thought she could be saved, however the French fleet attacked Hastings and Rye on 5 July and her captain decided to burn the *Anne* to avoid her being taken as a prize.

The Royal Military Canal was constructed between 1804 and 1809, and starts at Cliff End, Pett (TQ889135), before following the northern edge of Pett Level to Winchelsea. The work between Pett and Winchelsea was supervised by Lt. Colonel Nicolay who used civilian labour to dig the canal and soldiers to build the ramparts and other defence works.

In May 1940 three gaps were cut in the sea wall at Pett Level to flood the levels as a protective measure to deter any German landing. Anti-tank pimples and other anti-tank obstacles were positioned along the beach at Cliff End and were supported with barbed wire and other defensive positions. Scaffolding was also positioned along the entire frontage at medium tide level. The gaps in the sea wall were closed again in 1944.

An Emergency Coastal Battery was located on Toot Rock (TQ893137) overlooking the beach and comprised two 6in BL Mk16 guns and two searchlights. This battery was manned by 105 Coast Battery initially and then 374 Coast Battery, part of 551 Coast Regiment RA.

A single Type 22 pillbox was located by The Royal Military Canal, probably serving a dual purpose in protecting the flank of the battery whilst also covering the open ground across the Levels.

In April 1944 a QL decoy site No. 654 was established at Pett Level (TQ895138) as part of the D-Day deception plan Fortitude South. It was erased in August after it had served its purpose.

The sites today

Substantial remains of the Emergency Coastal Battery on Toot Rock have survived and can be seen on the high ground some 200m to the rear of the beach. A two-storey brick and concrete observation post (OP) stands at the west end of Toot Rock (TQ 8914 1371). It has an entrance and window in the north wall at ground floor level and originally steps inside would have led to the upper floor where a mount for the range finding equipment is still in situ. On the east side of the OP is a concrete block with a holdfast (*colour plate 15*) perhaps for mounting a light anti-aircraft weapon or more likely a searchlight. To the west of the OP is the remains of a circular anti-aircraft gun position (TQ 8912 1369), enclosed by a low wall constructed from hollow concrete blocks. Some 30m to the rear of the OP is the base for a spigot mortar (TQ 8913 1374). This comprises a steel pin mounted on an irregularly shaped concrete block, and was located here to provide local defence for the battery (*40*). A possible circular weapons pit can be seen on the front edge of Toot Rock between the OP and gun position.

Further east at TQ 8918 1376, one of the gun positions has survived. The open areas are overgrown, but it is possible to discern the gun floor, with covered ammunition recesses and the war shelter to its rear. Offset to one side is the covered shell and cartridge store, with a trapdoor entrance and ladder. There is no trace of the second gun position, which was located further east, as it is now below one of the bungalows. Further concrete bases can be seen at the rear of Toot Rock at TQ 8909 1372 and probably mark the location of other buildings associated with the battery.

There is no sign of the pillbox near the Royal Military Canal, which is apparently still extant, but totally overgrown. On the beach at Cliff End (TQ 8885 1310) amongst a tumble of concrete fragments, are a number of anti-tank pimples and occasional anti-tank buoys and cylinders. These are the remains of the obstacles that were located here until after the 1987 storms, when they were uprooted to make way for new anti-erosion coastal defences.

40 The base for a spigot mortar, Pett Level (TQ 8913 1374). Note the steel pin mount for the spigot mortar on an irregularly shaped concrete block, which was located here to provide local defence for the ECB

Directions and access

Take the A259 from Hastings to Winchelsea, and after 1km turn into Pett Road. Follow this to Pett, and then continue on to Cliff End. At the T-junction, turn left and after 200m park in the small car park on the right. From the car park walk along the Saxon Shore Way eastwards (following the Royal Military Canal), and the OP can be seen on Toot Rock to your left. After visiting the battery, continue to the footpath junction by a bridge over the Royal Military Canal, then turn right and cross the road.

Here you will find a sign board telling the story of the *Anne*. Further information on the *Anne* can be found in the Hastings Shipwreck Heritage Centre (see Site 23) and the wreck can sometimes be seen at very low tides.

Return by walking along the seafront. This will take you to the uprooted pimples on the beach at Cliff End.

References/Background reading

Dobinson, C. 2000, *Fields of Deception*, London, Methuen Publishing Ltd

Hutchinson, G. 1995, *The Royal Military Canal: A Brief History*, Hastings, M & W Morgan

Longstaff-Tyrrell, P. 2002, *Tyrrell's List*, Polegate, Gote House Publishing

Mace, M.F. 1997, *Sussex Wartime Relics and Memorials*, Storrington, Historic Military Press

Marsden, P. 1987, *The Historic Shipwrecks of South-East England*, Norwich, Jarrold and Sons Ltd

SITE 26: WINCHELSEA

Period: **Napoleonic and Second World War**
Type of site: **Gun battery, pillboxes and anti-tank obstacles**

History

An earthwork feature called 'The Old Battery' is shown on early Ordnance Survey maps and was probably constructed during the Napoleonic Wars to provide support for the adjacent Royal Military Canal.

The first line of defence here in 1940 was at Winchelsea Beach on the coast, whilst Winchelsea town itself became a Category A Nodal Point. The Levels between Winchelsea Beach and Pett were flooded and the beach was lined with anti-tank obstacles and other defences, whilst the entire population of Winchelsea Beach was evacuated. An observation post (OP) was built on the higher ground at TQ 9178 1628 and was part of the Emergency Coastal Battery which was located on the shore at TQ918160. This battery had two 6in BL MkVII guns and two DEL (searchlights) in 1945.

A number of machine gun emplacements were located at Winchelsea Beach and along Nook Beach towards Rye Harbour. Further back from the beach, a number of pillboxes were constructed on the high ground overlooking the Royal Military Canal; others covered Strand Bridge, and then continued the line north-eastwards along the River Brede towards Rye. Some of these are only known from a German map of 1941. The public house located near Strand Bridge was also apparently fortified.

The sites today

The Old Battery can still be seen as a discrete triangular earthwork at TQ 9109 1751 on the north side of the River Brede, close to its junction with the Royal Military Canal.

The three-storey brick and concrete OP at Winchelsea Beach survives today in the garden of one of the houses in Smeatons Lane. The first storey is reached by wooden steps and has two small windows and internal steps up to the second storey. This upper storey had a continuous narrow window along the front wall and part way along both side walls. A concrete base in one corner probably provided the mount for the range finding equipment. The ground floor is partially sunken into the mound and was used as a machine gun emplacement. It is entered by steps from ground level and has two narrow embrasures facing east and west, which still have metal weapon mounts in situ. There is an internal Y-shaped blast wall and cabling ducts enter the OP through the walls at this level.

Nothing else of the Emergency Coastal Battery can be seen. However, a little further north along Dogs Hill Lane are two small brick buildings with concrete roofs, now used as garages. These are associated with bungalows that would have been requisitioned for the battery personnel and these buildings may have been part of the battery domestic site. At the sea wall end of Dogs Hill Lane there are 18 anti-tank buoys lining the edge of the road (TQ 9180 1607), together with some large rectangular blocks which may be from the post-war sea defences.

A rectangular wooden-shuttered concrete machine gun emplacement survives at TQ 9172 1666, to the north of the OP. It has an almost continuous narrow embrasure, with steps down to an entrance on its west side. It appears to be used as a fire hydrant and cannot be accessed due to a padlocked door. A second similar emplacement is located at the west end of The Ridge (TQ 9207 1852), and a third very damged emplacement is situated on the edge of the water-filled quarry near Watch House (TQ 9281 1744).

Only three of the other Winchelsea pillboxes are still extant. The first occupies a hilltop vantage point adjacent to Wickham Rock Lane between Winchlesea and Icklesham (TQ 8938 1610) and has a superb view over Pett Levels. It is an unusual square concrete emplacement, with a large open embrasure facing south-east, that also provides a sizeable concrete table. At the rear there is a narrow entrance with a blast wall and roof forming a porch. It has no surviving weapons mount or holdfast and may therefore have served as an observation post.

The second pillbox is located beside the A259 road between Winchelsea and Rye, at TQ 9157 1814. This is a concrete machine gun emplacement set into the

41 Type 22 pillbox situated on a raised piece of ground overlooking the River Brede at Winchelsea (TQ 9166 1755)

rear slope of the riverbank. It has a large embrasure in each wall, although three were then blocked up, leaving just one facing south-east across the river towards Camber Castle. It has an entrance on the north-west side and inside there are tables for mounting Vickers machine guns at three of the embrasures (two of which are blocked).

The third pillbox is situated to the south of the previous emplacement on a bend in the River Brede (TQ 9166 1755). It is a Type 22 pillbox with an external blast wall and sits on a raised piece of ground facing across the river to the south-east (*41*).

In Winchelsea Town there is little surviving evidence for its use as a Nodal Point. A single anti-tank buoy is located on the corner of Mill Road and the A259.

Directions and access

Winchelsea Beach is reached by taking Sea Road from the A259 at Strand Bridge. The Royal Military Canal can be seen on the right immediately after this junction, but the Old Battery site cannot be seen from the road. Follow Sea Road for 2km then take the left fork into Dogs Hill Road and park at the small car park at the sea wall to see the anti-tank buoys. The OP is a short walk along Smeatons Lane, but is on private land with no access, and can therefore only be viewed from the Lane. The machine gun emplacement north of the OP can be found by taking the footpath from Sea Road along Willow Lane; at Harbour Farm take the right-hand fork and the emplacement is at the junction with Morlains Ridge. To find the other two emplacements follow The Ridge east from the seafront, and continue following the footpath to Watch House.

To find the Icklesham emplacement, take the road south out of Winchlesea Town and at the sharp corner 100m before joining the A259, turn left into Wickham Rock Lane. Follow this through Winchelsea New Gate and after 0.75km there is a footpath on the left. Follow this across the field to the corner of the wood where the emplacement, which is on private land, can be seen. The machine gun emplacement between Winchelsea and Rye is on the south side of the A259 at a sharp corner. There is no parking along this busy road and the emplacement is on private land. The Type 22 pillbox is also on private land, but it can be viewed from the corner of Sea Road.

References/Background reading

Hutchinson, G. 1995, *The Royal Military Canal: A Brief History*, Hastings, M & W Morgan

Saville, M. & R 2006, *A Changing Shore*, Hastings, Edgerton Publishing Service

Defence of Britain Database (LuftflottenKommando2 1941/01/12)

ESCC SMR record: ES7238-MES7238

SITE 27: CAMBER CASTLE

Period: **Tudor and Second World War**
Type of site: **Artillery fort and decoy site**

History

Construction of Camber Castle was begun in 1512-14 by Sir Edward Guldeford and comprised a round blockhouse 20m across, with gun ports to defend the mouth of the River Rother. Between 1539 and 1540 Henry VIII strengthened the site, by increasing the height of the blockhouse, which became a central keep, and surrounding it with an octagonal court, which was entered by a rectangular gatehouse on the north-west side. The court was enclosed by a double wall, and from the vaulted passageway between these walls, passages led out into four small D-shaped towers. Further modifications in 1542-3, added more height to the central keep: a D-shaped addition to the outside of the gatehouse and four large D-shaped bastions were added to the outside. At some stage, probably in the early seventeenth century, the north and south bastions were filled to create 'dead mounts' for artillery pieces and a rampart was created in the south-east quadrant of the castle for the same purpose. A man-made earthwork is visible outside the castle on its south and east sides, and was probably constructed to provide defence against the sea.

The garrison comprised eight soldiers and six gunners in 1544, with the number of gunners rising to 17 by 1550, with 26 or 28 cannon of various types. From 1568 ten guns were located at Camber Castle, with six bronze cannon being replaced with six iron cannon in 1593. By the 1620s the Rother had migrated out

42 In the background is the Stanton shelter that formed the control shelter for the decoy site at Camber Castle, with the partly demolished generator building in the foreground

of range of the castle's guns, and having outlived its purpose, the garrison was disbanded in 1637. In 1642 the guns were removed and the castle was dismantled by Parliamentary forces.

During the Second World War the area around the castle was utilised as a decoy site to divert German bombers from their real target, in this case Rye. Initially in July 1942 it was established as SF No. 78, and in May 1944 it changed to a QL site No. 651 as part of the D-Day deception plan *Fortitude South*, before being abandoned in February 1945.

The sites today

The castle is situated at TQ922185 within the Rye Harbour Nature Reserve and is now in the care of English Heritage (*colour plate 1*). Although it has lost its roof, enough of the castle remains to provide a good impression of how it would have looked originally.

At TQ 9183 1881 stands a concrete Stanton shelter, with alongside it a partly dismantled structure with three large holes perforating its wall (*42*). Nearby is the concrete base for a demolished brick building, and a further area of concrete. These are the remains of the decoy site, with the Stanton shelter originally serving as the control shelter and the partly dismantled structure being the generator building.

Directions and access

Park in Rye and visit the information centre in Strand Quay, where you can pick up the *Camber Castle Walk* leaflet, which takes you on a circular route taking in both the castle and the decoy site.

Opening times
Camber Castle is managed by the Rye Harbour Nature Reserve for English
Heritage.

It is open 1 July-30 September between 2pm-5pm on Saturdays and Sundays
only, and also over the May bank holiday weekend. At other times it can only be
viewed externally.

Telephone: 01797 223862

References/Background reading

Dobinson, C. 2000, *Fields of Deception*, London, Methuen Publishing Ltd
Salter, M. 2000, *The Castles of Sussex*, Malvern, Folly Publications
Biddle, M., Hiller, J., Scott, I. and Streeten, A. 2001, *Henry VIII's Coastal Artillery
    Fort at Camber Castle, Rye, East Sussex*, London, English Heritage

SITE 28: RYE

Period: **Tudor to Second World War**
Type of site: **Gun batteries, Martello Tower and Nodal Point**

History

Ypres Tower was probably built in the fourteenth century and became the focus
for the town's defences. It had three floors and was built into the town wall. The
Tower was bought by the town corporation in 1518 and was used as the town
prison until 1865.

In Tudor times Rye had a large estuary and harbour, being able to shelter large
numbers of ships in the Wainway, and became the largest and busiest port on the
south coast. Rye became a major point of embarkation for Henry VIII's army in
1513 and again in 1544 for his Boulogne expedition. Repairs were carried out
on the town's defences in 1522-3 with guns being placed on the Strand, on the
Landgate and on a platform on the cliff. More preparations were undertaken in
1544-5 to make the walls fit to hold ordnance, developing the Gun Garden and
constructing a new fortress at the Strand.

In 1562 Rye was the point of embarkation for Elizabeth I's Le Havre expedition.
However by 1570 there were complaints that the harbour was silting up and in
1580 two groynes were built to try to resolve the problem. A map of 1572 shows
Rye to be well-provisioned with cannon. At the time of the Armada in 1588 Rye
had to provide a single ship (The *William* of 60 tons) and the town's defences
were improved with the restoration of the Gun Garden.

In 1603 the town walls were intact and the battery at the Gun Garden and the
Strand still held some guns; however, Rye was declining in importance due to the

silting up of the harbour. In 1689 there were three guns at Castle Point and one at Gun Garden rocks, all of which appear to have been in a state of disrepair, and by 1698 the Commissioners of the Navy concluded 'the harbour to be almost entirely lost'. In 1741 eight cannons were placed in the Gun Garden and in 1779 five new brass cannon (captured from the Spanish) were put on the green.

During the Napoleonic Wars Martello Tower 30 was built at Rye to defend the sluices of the Royal Military Canal and the Rivers Brede and Tillingham. The tower was moated and also had a wet ditch that surrounded the bank into which the tower and moat was dug. There was also a plan to flood the low-lying land around Rye. Local volunteers raised in Rye during the Napoleonic Wars included the 3rd Battalion of the Cinque Ports Volunteer Corps and the Rye Battery of Artillery.

In 1858 during the Napoleon III invasion scare, Rifle Volunteers and a Volunteer Artillery unit were formed at Rye. By 1873 the Martello Tower was not armed, but was retained for use as a magazine. At some stage during the nineteenth century the Gun Garden battery appears to have been modified with two pivot mounts, one at each end. Between them were five other gun positions and to the rear a loopholed wall.

The First World War appears to have had little visible impact on Rye, but during the Second World War Rye became a Nodal Point and was heavily defended from all directions. From the east, Monkbretton Bridge, that carries the A259 over the River Rother, was prepared for demolition and a roadblock comprised of concrete blocks was placed across the road. The blocks had slots for horizontal steel rails and 'hairpin' rails that fitted into slots in the road, and was supplemented by anti-tank cylinders and buoys. The bridge was also covered by a pillbox located by the Fishmarket (approximately TQ924206 – demolished in the 1970s). The railway bridge over the Rother, just to the north of Monkbretton Bridge, was also prepared for demolition and covered by a pillbox. Other pillboxes were positioned to cover the approach from Camber and the River Rother between Rye Harbour and Rye.

Three pillboxes covered the River Brede frontage, one between the River Rother and Rock Channel (approximately TQ 9245 2035 – removed in the 1960s), one at Rock Channel House and the third by the Sluice Keepers Cottage at Brede Sluice. On the west side of Rye, Tillingham Bridge (A259) and sluice was covered by a sunken bunker with embrasures at ground level. This latter bunker was camouflaged as a grassy knoll, whilst the other pillboxes were camouflaged as sheds using timber sections taken from holiday homes at Camber and Winchelsea Beach.

On the northern side of the town an anti-tank barrier was created to complete the defensive ring. Starting at the River Tillingham four rows of anti-tank pimples climbed up Leasam Hill to the A268, then followed New England Lane down to the Military Road and then on to the bank of the River Rother. Other pimples were located on the bank of the Rother and in Deadmans Lane, while the A268 and Military Road could be closed with anti-tank cylinders and buoys.

43 The Gun Garden at Rye with Ypres Tower in the background. Note the loopholed wall to the rear of the battery, which was added in the nineteenth century

Within the perimeter were two 25pdr field gun detachments, located in Tillingham Avenue and in a field to the rear of South Undercliff. Other guns were located near to the Rother Iron Works covering the approach to Rye Harbour.

A small number of 40mm Bofors guns were provided for anti-aircraft defence at the start of the war and numerous public air-raid shelters were constructed throughout the town in 1939. Other shelters were built at schools and two underground shelters were constructed at the railway station. There were also a number of underground private shelters and numerous Anderson shelters were provided. In 1944 Operation Diver resulted in two batteries, each of eight HAA guns, being added to the town's defences.

The sites today

Ypres Tower and the Gun Garden (TQ 9226 2025) in the centre of the town are open to the public, with a number of replica cannon mounted in positions in the Gun Garden to represent a nineteenth-century battery (*43*).

Martello Tower 30 does not appear to have been used during the Second World War and was converted to a residence shortly afterwards. It is now standing derelict and is covered in ivy.

A number of Second World War defence installations survive around the town. At Monkbretton Bridge, all trace of the roadblock has disappeared, although a single anti-tank cylinder survives as a gatepost on the west side of the bridge

44 An impressive group of anti-tank pimples located in the grounds of the ambulance station at Playden, Rye

(TQ 9242 2066). The Type 22 pillbox covering the railway bridge is situated at TQ 9243 2083. It is constructed from concrete blocks and has both external and internal blast walls. Of the other pillboxes, a Type 22 of concrete block construction with an internal blast wall survives in the garden of Rock Channel House (TQ 9231 2006), overlooking the River Brede, whilst a second Type 22 can be found at the Sluice Keepers Cottage at Brede Sluice (TQ 9194 1989). This is also constructed from concrete blocks and sits on a 12in-thick concrete foundation. Its internal blast wall has been removed and in the recent past it has been put to various uses including an aviary. The underground bunker covering the Tillingham Bridge has been covered over and is located adjacent to the Strand Café beneath the road sign (TQ 9174 2026).

Of the northern defences, some 34 anti-tank pimples survive in the grounds of the ambulance station at Playden (TQ 9193 2155), adjacent to the A268. Remains of four rows of pimples can be seen, approximately 4ft apart, approaching the road, and then a single line at 90° to these along the side of the road (*44*). Others apparently survive in gardens along the route of the original line.

There is little evidence for the Bofors and artillery positions around the town, however, a Nissen hut hidden amongst the undergrowth after the last house on the New Winchelsea Road (A259) may mark the location of one Bofors gun position (approximately TQ916191). A surface air-raid shelter can also be found at No. 6 Wish Street (TQ 9182 2034). It has been incorporated into the later house, forming the ground floor, but can be recognised due to the lack of any windows at this level.

Of the defences outside Rye, a single machine gun emplacement survives adjacent to the lake at Northpoint Beach on the Camber Road (TQ 9317 2021). This is similar to the emplacements at Frenchman's Beach, Rye Harbour (see Site 27), and is constructed from wooden-shuttered concrete, with a narrow continuous embrasure separated into six sections by a number of vertical concrete divisions. There is an entrance on the north side and inside there is a continuous shelf with a double slot for mounting the machine gun(s).

Directions and access

There are numerous car parks in Rye town centre, from which all of the sites can be reached. The Martello Tower is located in Martello Close (a private road) and there is no access to the tower itself.

The pillbox at the railway bridge can be found by walking along the footpath north from Monkbretton Bridge. The Type 22 pillbox at Rock Channel House is on private property and cannot be seen, however, the Type 22 at the Sluice Keepers Cottage can be found by walking down Harbour Road opposite Martello Close; it is on the left immediately before the Sluice. It is best viewed from Harbour Road on the opposite side of the River Brede.

The anti-tank pimples at Playden can be found by taking the A268 to Peasmarsh from Rye town centre. The ambulance station is on the left side of the road after 1km and the pimples are on the grassed area behind the hedge. Parking is difficult on the main road and there is no vehicle access into the ambulance station.

The machine gun emplacement at Northpoint Beach can be visited by parking in the small layby on the Camber Road, adjacent to the Rye Water Sports centre. Walk west towards Rye along the cycleway for 300m and then turn left at the stile just before the bridge; the emplacement is 30m in front of you.

Opening times

Rye Castle Museum is located in the Ypres Tower, which has limited opening hours and between 1 November and 31 March is only open at weekends. There is an admission charge. Details can be obtained on 01797 226728 or from their website below.

References/Background reading

Kirkham, J. 2002, *Rye's War*, Rye, Rye Museum Association

Mayhew, G.J. 1984, 'Rye and the Defence of the Narrow Seas: A 16th Century Town at War', *Sussex Archaeological Collections* 122, 107-26

PRO WO33/25

www.martello-towers.co.uk
www.ryemuseum.co.uk

SITE 29: RYE HARBOUR

Period: **Napoleonic to Second World War**
Type of site: **Martello Tower and machine gun emplacements**

History

Two Martello Towers were constructed at Rye Harbour. The first (No. 28 – also known as the Enchantress Tower) was constructed within a dry moat with an earth and shingle bank built up around the moat-retaining brick wall (*45*). The tower was built from both yellow and red bricks, and rendered externally. Little is known of its early history, but in 1873 it was armed with a 7in Armstrong Gun, and in the 1930s it may have been used as a Coastguard station. The second tower (No. 29) was located near Rye Harbour mouth, and was lost to coastal erosion in the 1820s.

During the Second World War a number of machine gun emplacements were constructed at Rye Harbour; two were located near to the mouth of the harbour, whilst others were located further back around Rye Harbour village. These emplacements were supported by other defence works, minefields and barbed wire, together with beach scaffolding, which was positioned at medium tide level along the beach. Other anti-tank obstacles would have blocked the access from the beach towards Rye.

An artillery position and searchlight was located near Lime Kiln Cottage covering the harbour entrance. During Operation Diver a Z Battery was located near to Martello Tower 28.

45 Martello Tower No. 28 (also known as the Enchantress Tower) at Rye Harbour; covered with ivy and sitting within its dry moat

The sites today

Martello Tower 28 sits within its dry moat at TQ 9418 1885. The tower is in a derelict condition, largely overgrown with ivy and has lost most of its rendering. Some sections of the moat-retaining wall are exposed, where the bank has been removed.

The concrete machine gun emplacements at Rye Harbour appear to have been unique to this area (*46*). The two emplacements at the entrance to Rye Harbour (at TQ 9485 1797 and TQ 9491 1817) are rectangular with six wide embrasures, each fronting a concrete table for a Vickers machine gun. On each front corner is a narrow horizontal slot and the door is in the north wall adjacent to one of the embrasures. The emplacement nearest to the shore has a camouflaged shingle roof (*colour plate 16*).

Two other machine gun emplacements of a different variety are located within the Frenchman's Beach holiday village, close to the Martello Tower at TQ 9419 1873 and TQ 9406 1864. They are rectangular concrete emplacements, smaller than those at the harbour entrance, with a continuous narrow embrasure separated into six sections by a number of vertical divisions. Both emplacements have an entrance on the west side with an external blast wall for protection. A similar emplacement survives at Northpoint Beach (see Site 28).

A large concrete base, located close to Lime Kiln Cottage on the west bank of the River Rother (TQ 9458 1860) is probably the remains of the gun position protecting the harbour entrance.

46 Machine gun emplacement at Rye Harbour (TQ 9491 1817) with the second emplacement on the shingle beach in the background

In Rye Harbour village four anti-tank cylinders line the edge of the road in front of the houses, whilst at least another 12 can be found lying on the grass opposite (TQ 9423 1907); others may be buried here. These probably originate from a nearby roadblock.

Directions and access

From Rye follow Harbour Road to Rye Harbour where there is a large car park. The Martello Tower is adjacent to the car park, while permission to visit the two machine gun emplacements within the Frenchman's Beach holiday village should be requested at the reception centre near the entrance. A footpath to the harbour entrance takes you past Lime Kiln Cottage, where there is a small information centre; continue past this to find the emplacements located at the entrance.

References/Background reading

Kirkham, J. 2002, *Rye's War*, Rye, Rye Museum Association

Kirkham, J. 2006, *Bygone Rye Harbour*, (2nd ed.), Rye, Thomas Peacocke School Local History Group

Russell, J. and Barber, L. 2005, *Pett Levels Pillbox, Rye Harbour, Rye, East Sussex*, Unpublished Report, Archaeology South-East

PRO WO33/25

SITE 30: CAMBER SANDS

Period: **Second World War**
Type of site: **Pillboxes and anti-tank obstacles**

History

In 1940 the broad, open, sandy beach at Camber Sands would have made an ideal landing place for the German invasion forces, giving them access to Rye and the Weald beyond. Rising up behind the beach are large sand dunes and it was in these dunes that a number of machine gun emplacements were constructed, covering the beach and paths through the dunes from the beach. Anti-tank cubes lined the beach and were supported by other defences such as barbed wire and minefields, whilst scaffolding was positioned along the entire frontage at medium tide level. The defending infantry were the 2nd Battalion of the Royal Sussex Regiment.

To the east of Camber at Broomhill Farm, fuel tanks were set into the rear of the sea wall road embankment and concrete bunkers with pumping equipment were co-located with them so that in the event of an invasion fuel could be pumped into the sea and set alight (Sea Flame Barrage). Further east at Jury's Gut Sluice (TQ990180) was an Emergency Coastal Battery with two or three 6in BL guns, manned initially by 213 Coast Battery and then later by 415 Coast Battery, part of 551 Coast Regiment RA.

During Operation Diver heavy anti-aircraft batteries (each of eight guns) were installed at Maddison's Holiday Camp at Camber and at Moneypenny Farm, East Guldeford.

The sites today

Seven concrete machine gun emplacements survive at Camber Sands, but two are now buried under the dunes and three others are inaccessible. The dunes are constantly moving and increasing in size, and have completely covered the two easternmost emplacements. The first of these is located to the north-west of the shops at the Central car park (approximately TQ966186) and is buried to a depth of some six to eight feet. The second is located a little further west at TQ964186 in the dunes between the marker posts F and G, and has been buried for two to three years now; no trace of it could be found in 2006. Both of these are the same type as the remaining emplacement, which can be found partly buried at TQ 9607 1870 where it covered the path between the beach and Old Lydd Road (47). These emplacements are square, with an entrance located in the north wall, protected by an integral blast wall. Each emplacement has a combination of narrow and wide embrasures, although these are now covered with sand on this last example, which is slowly disappearing into the sand dune.

A second group of three machine gun emplacements can be found further west, adjacent to the path between the Coastguard Cottages and the beach. Two are located within a few metres of each other on the west-facing slope of the dunes (TQ 9575 1875) covering the path. They are subsiding, surrounded by vegetation and cannot be approached. The third emplacement is on the west side of the path next to a golf tee on Rye Golf Course (TQ 9566 1877). This is constructed from wooden-shuttered concrete and is partly buried, but appears to have a bricked-up embrasure or door at its west end.

The final machine gun emplacement is located in the line of dunes within Rye Golf Course at TQ 9525 1894. It is a rectangular, wooden-shuttered, concrete emplacement measuring 28 x 13ft, on a corrugated iron-shuttered base, with some of the corrugated iron still in situ. It has six very narrow embrasures, two in each long side and one in each short end, and an entrance (now blocked) in its south-east wall. It has good views through 360° across the golf course.

Very little remains of the other beach defences at Camber Sands, as they were quickly cleared away after the war. However, at the entrance to the Central car park are the remains of a roadblock (TQ 9656 1866). This comprises two large 6ft sq concrete blocks, one on each side of the car park entrance. The block on the south-west side has three vertical slots, each of a different depth, whilst the north-east block has three matching rectangular holes, designed to take the horizontal metal rails that would have blocked the road. To the north-east of the roadblock are three smaller concrete cubes, whilst two similar cubes survive on the south-

47 Partly buried machine gun emplacement beside the path between the beach and Old Lydd Road at Camber Sands (TQ 9607 1870)

west side; these would have originally continued in both directions to prevent vehicles going around the roadblock. A further cube, with a pyramidal top, can be found between the shops and seaside chalets on the beach side of the Central car park (TQ 9566 1877); this is probably an in situ remnant of the original line of cubes along the beach.

At Broomhill Farm, two brick-shuttered concrete bunkers can be seen built into the rear of the road embankment, one on each side of the farm track, at TQ 9770 1834 and TQ 9774 1834. The first is overgrown and inaccessible; however, the second has an entrance on its north side, but is flooded inside. These probably held the equipment for pumping fuel into the sea, although the associated fuel tanks are no longer present. Continuing eastwards along Lydd Road from here, some 50-60 anti-tank buoys edge the road for the next 600m.

At Jury's Gut sluice, the remains of the domestic site associated with the Emergency Coastal Battery can be seen on the north side of the road (centred on TQ990181). Numerous concrete foundations and the remnants of brick walls can be seen in the undergrowth, whilst a complete rectangular brick building with double wooden doors can also be seen. Nearby are two anti-tank cylinders at the entrance to Jury's Gap (TQ 9908 1808) and a further seven anti-tank buoys are stored in the adjacent depot.

Directions and access
From Rye follow the Camber Road from the A259. Turn into Old Lydd Road and follow this until you reach the Central car park at the junction with Sea

Road. All of the surviving machine gun emplacements can be found by walking west along the beach and then into the dunes. Alternatively, park at the Western car park, which can be accessed from Camber Road. The first machine gun emplacement can be found beside the footpath to the beach from behind the toilet block at the east end of the car park. The second group of emplacements can be found by using the path to the beach from the west end of the car park, near to the Coastguard Cottages. The emplacement on the west side of the path can be reached through a gate onto the golf course. The two emplacements on the east side of the path cannot be reached, but can be clearly seen from the top of the high dune in the golf course. There is no access to the emplacement in the middle of the golf course, but it can be viewed from a lay-by on the Camber Road.

To find the sites at Broomhill Farm and Jury's Gut, take the Lydd Road east out of Camber. There are numerous car parks and lay-by's along this road. All of these sites are on private property.

Opening times
The accessible sites can be seen at any reasonable time. Both of the car parks in Camber require payment at the entrance.

References/Background reading
Kirkham, J. 2002, *Rye's War*, Rye, Rye Museum Association

www.combinedops.com/pluto.htm

3

THE GHQ STOP LINE

The GHQ Stop Line was created in 1940 as one of the major defence lines designed to block access to London and the rest of Britain from the south-east coasts of Kent and Sussex. It started at Newhaven on the south coast, then followed the River Ouse northwards to Uckfield, where it then took the line of the River Uck for a short distance before following the railway from Buxted to Crowborough. To the north of Crowborough the Stop Line continued to follow the railway as far as Groombridge on the Kent border, before finally taking the line of the River Medway into Kent.

The main defensive work on the Stop Line in Sussex was the Type 24 pillbox, although, along its route there are many minor variants of this type to see. Supplementing these, at road and railway bridges, is the Type 28 anti-tank pillbox, normally with a 6pdr holdfast, but again there are numerous variants to see. Occasionally along the line there are completely different types of pillbox. For example, around Crowborough there is a local variant that I have termed the 'Crowborough pillbox', of which at least six examples survive. At Buxted Park a unique machine gun emplacement survives and at Rise Farm to the south of Lewes there are three 'squashed' Type 24 variants. There are also short lengths of anti-tank ditch and occasional roadblocks that survive along its route.

One of the unique aspects of this Stop Line is the numbering of each pillbox. Each pillbox had a number prefixed by the letter 'A', which can normally be found on the internal blast wall facing the entrance. The numbering system starts at the north end of the line and continues down to Newhaven, where the highest number that survives today is A333 (Type 24 pillbox at Southease). This suggests that there must have originally been some 350 pillboxes along the Stop Line.

This chapter starts at Newhaven on the south coast and then follows the GHQ Stop Line northwards, and whilst concentrating on the Stop Line itself, also looks at the towns, Nodal Points and other sites that occur along its route.

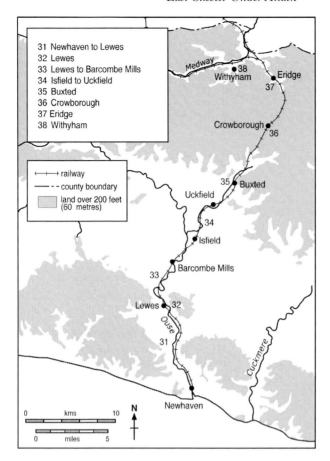

31 Newhaven to Lewes
32 Lewes
33 Lewes to Barcombe Mills
34 Isfield to Uckfield
35 Buxted
36 Crowborough
37 Eridge
38 Withyham

railway
county boundary
land over 200 feet
(60 metres)

48 GHQ Stop Line
map

SITE 31: NEWHAVEN TO LEWES

Period: **Second World War**
Type of site: **Pillboxes**

History

Newhaven town and harbour were protected by the coastal defence batteries located at the fort and on Castle Hill (Site 3). For local defence a number of pillboxes were constructed around the town, whilst barbed wire and anti-tank cubes lined the beaches. There were two pillboxes located at East Beach, one of which was a Type 28, supplemented by a 10 ton railway wagon containing a concrete casement with firing slits. There were also tanks and pumping equipment to pump fuel into the harbour, which would then be ignited in the event of an attack; photographs show the Sea Flame Barrage being tested in January 1942. The steam yacht, HMS *Schievan* was stationed at the harbour approaches as an inspection ship, whilst the *Davaar* was packed with explosives as a blockship. Other pillboxes were located near the road bridge and on either side of Denton Island, whilst another was located at the Mill Creek sluice. A number of surface and below-ground air-raid shelters were erected in the town, and at local schools.

The GHQ Stop Line began its route northward from Newhaven, following the line of the River Ouse, with pillboxes regularly spaced along the west bank of the river. Other pillboxes were occasionally placed to their rear to provide protection in depth and there were clusters of pillboxes around the villages of Southease, Rodmell and Iford forming local strong points.

At Southease, the bridge over the River Ouse was defended by an adjacent pillbox, whilst set back on the edge of the higher ground a Type 28 pillbox mounted a Hotchkiss 6pdr anti-tank gun. A Type 24 pillbox near the Old Rectory protected the rear and southern flank of the anti-tank pillbox, whilst a second Type 24 was located at the north end of North Bank. Three further Type 24 pillboxes protected the approaches into the village from the south-east, south and north, forming a strong point at this potential crossing place. On the opposite side of the river, at Baydean, south of Itford Farm, a pair of pipe mines was buried under the road (A26). During the war an Army camp was constructed on the north side of the Southease, close to the Old Rectory, and comprised some 20 Nissen huts. After the Army moved out, the camp housed German prisoners of war awaiting repatriation.

A little further north at Rodmell, three Type 24 pillboxes guarded the north-east approaches to the village, while at Northease Manor two more Type 24s covered a track from the Brooks. At Iford there were two clusters of three Type 24 pillboxes; the first group covered a track, with one pillbox set back to give the defence some depth. The second group covered the approaches to Swanborough Manor. Another pillbox, disguised as a tearoom with a verandah, was located to cover the Kingston to Lewes road.

The Brooks is the name given to the large open area of flood plain south of Lewes, from which two small hills (Upper Rise and Lower Rise) dominate the low-lying area which is criss-crossed by ditches and streams. A number of pillboxes were located on these hills (*colour plate 17*), creating strong points covering the River Ouse and the road and rail bridges at Southerham. One of the pillboxes here was disguised as a haystack.

Anti-aircraft guns were placed at Southease, Northease Farm and at Rise Farm, although some of these may have been short-term positions used during Operation Diver.

The sites today
There are few surviving sites in Newhaven town, although a possible pillbox exists on railway land to the east of the town at TQ 4508 0075, guarding Mill Creek sluice. A number of surface air-raid shelters survive in the town, one of which is situated in the car park of the Harbourside Hotel (previously the Sheffield Hotel) in South Road (TQ 4468 0065). It has a dividing internal wall, and has been modified post-war for use as a store. Two other surface shelters have

been incorporated into buildings within the Parker Pen site (TQ450013), whilst a below-ground shelter survives to the rear of Newhaven Boys School, now the Hillcrest Centre (TQ 4451 0106).

All of the pillboxes along the bank of the River Ouse between Newhaven and Lewes were removed shortly after the war by a local civilian contractor who was hired to undertake the task. The pillboxes that survive along the Stop Line here have suffered from neglect and the effects of time. Many have lost parts of their external brick shuttering, mostly due to root damage from ivy and other vegetation, whilst others have large cracks in the brickwork (*49*).

The group of pillboxes at Southease survive, with the Type 28 located at TQ 4246 0547 covering Southease Bridge. This pillbox is terraced into a bank and has a large, partly sunken, entrance in its rear wall protected by a low brick blast wall. It has an additional external holdfast that mounted a French 75mm gun situated a few metres to the north-east, together with some added brick walling on the same side of the pillbox, which originally provided a shelter for the gun crew. Some 500m further north at North Bank (TQ 4249 0599) a Type 24 pillbox (A326) is terraced into the top of the bank and faces east towards the river. A further Type 24 pillbox (A33?) is located along a track, past the Old Rectory, north from the centre of the village (TQ 4237 0541), and is very overgrown with ivy. The platforms for the Nissen huts can be seen on the east side of this track.

A Type 24 pillbox (A333) is located at the south-east corner of the village (TQ 4238 0505) facing east and has a ditch to its front. The two remaining Type 24 pillboxes are situated adjacent to the minor road from Newhaven to Lewes. The first (A332) is situated at the south-west corner of the village (TQ 4222 0505), facing south along the road. It sits behind a flint wall in the corner of a field, on a brick base terraced into the slope. The second (A331) sits at the north-west corner of the village in a garden and faces west towards the road (TQ 4220 0529).

At Rodmell three Type 24 pillboxes survive on the north and east sides of the village. The first is located in a field boundary (TQ 4190 0650) to the north of the village and faces north towards the Brooks. The second (A309) is situated on the south side of a track to the river (TQ 4213 0644). It has a ditch on its north and east sides, and much of its brick shuttering has fallen away. The final pillbox faces east and is located on high ground at the edge of a sports field near the church (TQ 4223 0633). It has been modified by the addition of a large door and is currently used for storage, having been incorporated into the wall around the sports field (*colour plate 18*).

Two Type 24 pillboxes are located at Northease Manor, between Rodmell and Iford. Pillbox A305 is located in the centre of a field at TQ 4118 0671 and faces north-east, whilst A306 is situated on the south side of a track at TQ 4125 0673 and faces east.

The Type 24 pillboxes at Iford are located to the east and north-east of the village, overlooking the Brooks. The southern group comprise A304 in the corner of a field (TQ 4137 0738) facing east and covering a track from the Brooks. To its

49 Type 24 pillbox A302 at Iford, positioned in a hedgeline at TQ 4108 0744 covering the rear of two other Type 24 pillboxes located closer to the river. Note how the brickwork shuttering has fallen away due to root damage

north A303 is located in the north-east corner of a wood, facing east, with a ditch on two sides (TQ 4137 0756). Located some 250m to the west and covering the rear of these is a third Type 24 pillbox (A302), positioned in a hedgeline at TQ 4108 0744 (*49*). The second group of three Type 24 pillboxes are located further north and to the east of Swanborough Manor. Distributed around Iford Farm and village are numerous anti-tank buoys, which presumably originated from a nearby roadblock. On the east side of the Kingston to Lewes road an overgrown Type 24 pillbox (A296) can just be made out in the hedge line (TQ 4023 0855).

At Rise Farm, six pillboxes survive. Two Type 24 pillboxes are situated on the eastern slope of Upper Rise, with A293 (TQ 4194 0871) facing north towards the bridges and A294 (TQ 4203 0875) facing east towards the river. Further south another Type 24 (A313) covers the northern approach to Rise Barn (TQ 4237 0818). On Lower Rise there are three 'squashed' Type 24 variant pillboxes. The first is situated on the eastern slope (TQ 4250 0790) and faces east with a superb field of fire towards the river and Beddingham (*colour plate 17*). The other two are set further back in a hedgeline, with one (at TQ 4245 0782) covering the southern slope and the other (at TQ 4242 0800) covering the northern slope. All three are partly sunken and have external blast walls protecting the entrances.

Directions and access

All of the surviving pillboxes on this stretch of the Stop Line are on private property, but the following can be visited or seen from adjacent public rights of way. At Southease A331 can be seen from the adjacent bus stop on the Newhaven to Lewes road, whilst A332 is 100m further south in the corner of a field overlooking the road. At Rodmell, the pillbox at the sports field can be found by taking the footpath gate south out of the National Trust car park and heading towards the sports pavilion. A309 is located a short distance along the bridleway heading east from the National Trust car park main entrance. Pillbox A305 at Northease can be seen from the adjacent public footpath that runs from Northease Manor to Iford. A296 can be seen in the hedge line of the Kingston to Lewes road; there is a small lay-by just to its south, near the road junction. None of the pillboxes at Iford, Swanborough or Rise Farm can be visited as they are all on private farmland, with no public access.

Opening times

Newhaven Historical Society runs a very interesting Local and Maritime Museum at Paradise Park, Newhaven, on the B2109 (Avis Road).
www.newhavenmuseum.co.uk

1 April–31 October: Every day 2.00–4.00pm
1 November–31 March: Saturday and Sunday 2.00–5.00pm

References/Background reading

Elliston, R.A. 1999, *Lewes at War 1939-1945*, 2nd ed., Seaford, S.B. Publications

Mason, P. 2007, 'Newhaven Prepares for War', *Newhaven Times*, Journal of the Newhaven Historical Society

U3A 1993, *Lewes Remembers The Second World War (1939-1945)*, Lewes U3A Publications

SITE 32: LEWES

Period: **Second World War**
Type of site: **Nodal Point and civil defence installations**

History

As well as being on the GHQ Stop Line, Lewes was in a strategic location due to its road and rail bridges over the River Ouse. It was also an important rail junction, and therefore was designated as a Nodal Point. Roadblocks were established at entry points into the town; these being located at The Snowdrop Inn in South Street, The Chalkpit Inn on the Offham Road, at Mill Road in Malling Street, at Ashcombe Lane on the Kingston Road and at the top of Falmer Hill. These roadblocks comprised anti-tank coffins, cubes and buoys, and were supplemented by a *flame fougasse* at each site.

A number of pillboxes were built in Lewes town and along the river as a continuation of the GHQ Stop Line. A Type 24 pillbox was located in the meadows west of the River Ouse at TQ424095 and another was further north at TQ422099. Cliff Bridge over the River Ouse in Lewes (TQ 4193 1024) was protected by three large anti-tank coffins on its west side and was also prepared for demolition with explosives placed in chambers in the western abutment. Two pillboxes also covered the bridge. The first was an anti-tank pillbox positioned on the lower part of School Hill on the pavement adjacent to properties 212/213 (TQ 4176 1026). This pillbox was painted to resemble the buildings and was very difficult to see, causing a major nuisance to the residents until its removal in 1944. The second pillbox was located in the entrance to the Goods Yard adjacent to the Old Tabernacle Church and covered the exit from the bridge.

Two pillboxes were located at the Prison. The first was at the main entrance sited to fire down Western Road and was camouflaged to match the knapped flint of the prison boundary wall. The second was on the north-east side of the prison, set into a bank and sited to cover Spital Road. There was also an OP and loophole in the southern boundary wall of the prison along Brighton Road. Other pillboxes were situated at the Pells (in Pelham Terrace, disguised as a café with toilets) and at Lewes racecourse (TQ393112). In the south-east corner of the Castle Bowling Green a small store was taken over by the Home Guard and used as a bomb store.

Anti-aircraft guns were placed at a number of locations around Lewes, including on top of the chalk pit at Offham and at Lewes Racecourse, with others situated on the Caburn (see Site 41) and at Southease and Rise Farm (Site 31). The 338th Searchlight Battery was located at Offham, with the soldiers billeted at Coombe Place.

The Observer Corps manned a post in the South Tower of Lewes Castle throughout the war, with reports being passed directly to the Horsham Observer Control Centre by telephone. A total of 12 Air-Raid Warden Posts were established throughout the town. Many of these were initially sandbagged positions, but these were later replaced by purpose-built brick and concrete structures, whilst others utilised existing buildings.

A firewatching system was set up in 1940, with some 52 firms in Lewes operating firewatching schemes. Firewatch observation posts were established at a number of locations in the town, including Southover Church Tower and the Fire Station training tower, whilst a purpose-built observation post was placed on the Town Hall roof. A number of Emergency Water Supply (EWS) tanks were installed around the town to provide a static water supply for the fire service.

Numerous air-raid shelters were constructed across the town. Most of the public shelters were surface shelters, whilst those at schools were normally trench shelters. Many households adapted their basements to shelters, whilst Anderson and Morrison shelters were also supplied. On the Landport estate, the covered passageways between the houses were utilised as shelters.

The sites today

None of the Lewes pillboxes survive today; most were demolished immediately after the war, whilst some were actually removed during the last years of the war. There is also little evidence of the other defences surviving. An anti-tank cube survived adjacent to the Snowdrop Inn into the 1950s, but has now gone. However, nearby at the junction of South Street and Cliffe High Street (TQ 4215 1027) 19 anti-tank buoys are used to edge a small car park. At the Chalkpit Inn (TQ 4014 1163) nothing remains of the roadblock, but a cut in the roadside bank just north of the pub, may be the site of a machine gun post.

There is no remaining evidence for the Observer Corps post in the South Tower of the castle, although a climb to the top gives you a good impression of this vantage point for spotting German aircraft. Nearby on the Castle Bowling Green a large depression in the south-east corner marks the location of the 100,000 gallon EWS tank and in the north-east corner occasional parch marks and sunken areas in the grass show the original location of two air-raid shelters. The Home Guard bomb store in the south-east corner still remains in use as a store for the Lewes Bowling Green Society (TQ 4143 1013).

Three Air-Raid Warden's Posts survive. No. 2 Post was located at Cliffe Corner and survives as part of 'The Nutty Wizzard Café' (TQ 4219 1028) on the corner of Cliffe High Street and South Street. The brick and concrete outline (*50*) of No. 8 Post can be seen in the flint wall in Western Road (TQ 4059 1005), whilst No. 9 Post was located in the now disused Gentleman's toilets at the junction of Paddock Road and White Hill (TQ 4135 1026). The firewatch observation tower on the roof of the council offices off Fisher Street (approximately TQ 4152 1018) also still exists.

A number of air-raid shelters also survive in Lewes. At the Pells the concrete roof and some brickwork of a shelter built into the bank can be seen at TQ 4130 1052, whilst a shelter built in Westgate Street survives today as a garage, situated between the YMCA and WI buildings (TQ 4125 1004). Air-raid shelters were also located in The Paddock (also known as Baxters Field), of which one survives at the Bradford Road end. Its entrance and roof can be seen within the grassed mound in the south-west corner at TQ 4098 1012. Another shelter at the Offham Road end has been demolished in recent years and no trace of it could be found in 2006. A shelter also survives in the grounds of the St Nicholas Centre (previously the playground of Western Road School). Most of the remaining shelters were removed shortly after the war, but others have been removed quite recently, such as the covered trench shelter at County Hall, St Anne's Crescent (TQ408099). There are also four Anderson shelters in use as garden sheds on the Haredean Allotments (*51*), off the Brighton Road at TQ 3992 0942. The covered passageways between the houses on the Landport estate, which were used as shelters, can still be seen today.

50 The brick and concrete outline of the Air-Raid Warden's No. 8 Post can be seen in the flint wall in Western Road, Lewes (TQ 4059 1005)

51 An Anderson shelter now used as a garden shed on the Haredean Allotments, Lewes TQ 3992 0942

Directions and access

Lewes is a very difficult town in which to park, but is easily accessible by train. A street map can be obtained from the Tourist Information Office in the centre of the town and all of the sites mentioned above are within easy walking distance, apart from the Chalkpit Inn at Offham, which is on the A275 north of Lewes.

All of the sites mentioned above can be visited or seen from adjacent public rights of way, apart from the Anderson shelters on the Haredean Allotments and the air-raid shelter at the St Nicholas Centre to which there is no access.

Opening times
Lewes Castle: 01273 486290

Open Tuesday-Saturday, 10.00am-5.30pm and Sunday, Monday and bank holidays, 11.00am-5.30pm. Closed on Mondays in January and 24-26 December. The castle itself closes at dusk during winter. Last admissions are 30 minutes before closing time.

References/Background reading

Elliston, R.A. 1999, *Lewes at War 1939-1945*, 2nd ed., Seaford, S.B. Publications

Greatorex, C. 2002, *An Archaeological Recording Brief maintained on groundworks undertaken at County Hall Campus, St Anne's Crescent, Lewes, East Sussex*, Unpublished report

U3A 1993, *Lewes Remembers The Second World War (1939-1945)*, Lewes U3A Publications

www.sussexpast.co.uk

SITE 33: LEWES TO BARCOMBE MILLS

Period: **Second World War**
Type of site: **Pillboxes and Nodal Point**

History

The line of Type 24 pillboxes continued north out of Lewes to Hamsey on the west bank of the river. The River Ouse took a large meander around the low spur on which Hamsey Church is located and a straight cut was made by the Ouse Navigation Company in the late eighteenth century cutting off the spur. The pillboxes follow the line of the cut rather than the river at this point, and then continue up the west side of the river into Barcombe parish. As well as those positioned close to the river, a number were set back from the river and protected the rear of the forward pillboxes, across the low-lying flood plain.

Barcombe Mills is an important location, as it is the first crossing point across the River Ouse to the north of Lewes. As well as the river, there was a network of channels and weirs that fed the mills that had stood here (the last mill was burnt down in 1939) and were crossed by five separate bridges. Some nine pillboxes cover these bridges, forming one of the most concentrated defensive areas in Sussex. The various watercourses form two islands upon which four of the pillboxes were situated, thus improving their defensive capabilities, while the remaining pillboxes are strung along the west bank of the river, or in some cases set back from the river.

In addition to the pillboxes, roadblocks, barbed wire and earthwork defences were utilised to improve the Barcombe Mills Nodal Point. The defending forces in 1940 were drawn from 5th Battalion Loyal Regiment and 16 Platoon of 16th (Lewes) Battalion Sussex Home Guard; both units had their headquarters in Barcombe Cross, situated to the west of the River Ouse. Barcombe Cross had grown up around a three-way road junction and the (now disused) railway station. In 1940 it was part of the Barcombe Mills Nodal Point and roadblocks, including anti-tank cylinders, were set up in the village.

The sites today

Three surviving Type 24 pillboxes can be seen between Lewes and Hamsey. The first (A275) is located at TQ 4082 1118, adjacent to the London to Eastbourne railway line. It faces the river, with a raised entrance and large base to counteract the likelihood of flooding in this low-lying position. The second pillbox (A271) is built into the bank of the cut at TQ 4093 1209. It is positioned to cover the cut and the open ground to the south of the Hamsey spur. The third (A270) is located at TQ 4104 1228, in the appropriately named 'Pillbox Field' (52). This location, set back from the cut, enables it to cover both the rear of pillbox A271 and the bridge over the cut onto the Hamsey spur. This brick-shuttered Type 24 pillbox still retains its metal hinges and a catch for the door.

Ten pillboxes survive along the River Ouse from Hamsey to Barcombe Mills. They are all brick-shuttered Type 24 pillboxes, numbered A267 near Hamsey to A257, south of Barcombe Mills. One Pillbox (A262) was blown up and destroyed, probably by Canadian engineers during the war, and the blast wall of one of the surviving pillboxes (A260) has also been damaged, possibly by an explosion.

All of the pillboxes at Barcombe Mills survive today and provide an excellent example of a defended locality in its original setting. Some of the associated landscape has changed since the war – the railway line is now disused, but its embankment is still extant, flood defence improvements have raised the levees alongside the river and the reservoir is new. The new road bridge (Pikes Bridge) and current route of the road was apparently constructed later in the Second World War to take the increased road traffic prior to D-Day and therefore should be ignored when attempting to understand the 1940 defences.

Immediately south of Barcombe Mills are three Type 24 pillboxes that formed part of the defences at Barcombe Mills. Firstly A255, which was built against the

52 A Type 24 pillbox (A270) in the appropriately named 'Pillbox Field' at Hamsey (TQ 4104 1228), located to cover the bridge to Hamsey Church and the rear of the adjacent pillbox A271

railway embankment at TQ 4291 1482 and covers the river and the western flank of the pillboxes on the islands. The second pillbox (A256) is located 300m further south on a bend in the river at TQ 4278 1448. It is positioned on slightly higher ground and faces north-east covering the river and open ground to Barcombe Mills. The third pillbox (A254) is located to the rear of the Barcombe Mills position, at TQ 4283 1499. Situated on the high ground at the sharp bend in the road, it looks south-east and covers the rear of the railway embankment as well as the road.

A Type 28 anti-tank pillbox (A252) at TQ 4328 1482, with an adjacent Type 24 (A253) at TQ 4324 1483 protecting its western flank, was positioned on one of the islands covering the easternmost bridges (*colour plate 19*). Both of these pillboxes are bricked-up, but the Type 28 appears to have a holdfast for a 6pdr anti-tank gun. It has been suggested that the concrete and brick structure located to the rear of these pillboxes may be a buried command post.

Two Type 24 pillboxes (A250 and A251) were positioned on an adjacent island. Both face south and would have covered the approach to the bridges whilst also protecting the eastern flank of the Type 28 pillbox. The first (A250) is located at TQ 4351 1478 and is partly revetted into higher ground on the edge of a field with a ditch to its front. The second (A251) is situated at the edge of a field at TQ 4341 1477. Going north along track on the west bank of the river are further Type 24 pillboxes, of which the first two are an integral part of the Barcombe Mills Nodal Point. A249 is located in the grounds of Barcombe House (approximately

53 Some 60 anti-tank cylinders have been gathered together and arranged in a broad semi-circle forming a wall outside Gipps Farm (TQ 4319 1912) near Barcombe

TQ435149), set slightly back from the river, while A248 is in a hedge line at TQ 4359 1512, set back from the river. Further north, A247 is situated on some high ground on the west side of the track, behind a pond, at TQ 4379 1555, with a good view eastwards across the river.

Nine anti-tank cylinders survive in the centre of Barcombe Cross at the junction of School Lane and the School Hill/Spithurst Road (TQ 4206 1588). These were probably originally used in a roadblock at the adjacent road junction. Other cylinders have been collected up and repositioned at Gipps Farm, where some 60 cylinders are arranged in a broad semi-circle forming a wall at TQ 4319 1912 (*53*). Another two cylinders are located at the entrance to the wood yard opposite Sutton Hall at TQ 4329 1883.

Directions and access
The Hamsey pillboxes can be reached by turning off the A275 at Offham Church into The Drove and then turning right into Ivor's Lane after the level crossing. A270 is on private land, but can be viewed from the road. Take the footpath south towards Lewes alongside the cut to reach the other two pillboxes. A271 is reached after 350m, whilst A275 is a further kilometre; both of these can be visited.

From the A26 some 3km north of Lewes, take the minor road signposted to Barcombe. After one kilometre there is a car park on the right (closed in winter), or alternatively park on the verge near Pikes Bridge. From the car park walk to the bridges and turn right along a path between the first and second bridges to find pillboxes A251 and A250. Return to the bridges and turn right, past the tollhouse and follow the path to the left. A gate on your left leads into a field in which A252 and A253 are located. Follow the road to Mill Farm and join the footpath northwards. A248 is in a field on your left and can be viewed from the road; A249 is in the grounds of Barcombe House and cannot be accessed, though it can be seen through the trees from the east side of the river. A247 is difficult to see from the footpath as it is covered in ivy and is best viewed from the disused railway on its west side. Of the pillboxes to the south, only A254 can be visited as it is on a public footpath. A255 is on private property but can be seen from the road near Pikes Bridge and there is no access to A256. The remaining pillboxes between Hamsey and Barcombe Mills are all on private land, with no public access, and cannot be visited without first obtaining permission.

The anti-tank cylinders in Barcombe Cross are located in the centre of the village adjacent to the mini-roundabout. The other cylinders are located to the north of Barcombe Cross. Take the Spithurst Road and travel north for some three kilometres. The wood yard is on the left, opposite the entrance to Sutton Hall; Gipps Farm is a further 300m on the left. Parking is limited at both locations.

References/Background reading

Foot, W. 2006, *Beaches, fields, streets and hills: the anti-invasion landscapes of England*, CBA Research Report 144, York, Council for British Archaeology

Mace, M.F. 1997, *Sussex Wartime Relics and Memorials*, Storrington, Historic Military Press

SITE 34: ISFIELD TO UCKFIELD

Period: **Second World War**
Type of site: **Pillboxes**

History

The next group of pillboxes are situated near to the Anchor Inn, where a small bridge crossed the River Ouse. Two Type 24 pillboxes covered the bridge and sluices located here and a little further north a Type 28A pillbox covered the railway bridge across the river. Further Type 24 pillboxes were then placed at regular intervals along the River Ouse as far as the junction with the River Uck near Isfield Church. From here the main Stop Line follows the Uck eastwards to the north of Isfield and then turns north to Uckfield, with pillboxes located along the river and with a small group of pillboxes concentrated around Isfield Bridge. Roadblocks were located on all of the north–south roads, at bridges or at other appropriate choke points. These would have incorporated coffins, cylinders and buoys, with barbed wire and probably sandbagged fire positions.

A Royal Engineer camp was located at Isfield, with a siding coming off the Uckfield–Lewes railway line at Isfield station, whilst to the north of Uckfield a large army camp, originating in the First World War, was located at Maresfield.

The sites today

Many of the pillboxes along this stretch of the GHQ Stop Line survive. Near the Anchor Inn are two Type 24 pillboxes; one (A245) is located to the south of Anchor Lane in a hedge line between the river and the railway line (TQ 4398 1599). The second (A244) is to the north of Anchor Lane and backs onto the railway line, covering the open ground to the river (TQ441 161). This latter pillbox is of interest as two different types of bricks have used for its external shuttering. Further north is a Type 28A anti-tank pillbox (A243) located on a field boundary (TQ 4422 1644); this has a holdfast for a 6pdr gun, with a large entrance in its rear wall and a machine gun compartment on its south side (54).

Further north, on the line of the River Ouse, are another four Type 24 pillboxes (A242-A239). However, on reaching the junction with the River Uck, the pillboxes now follow the Uck past Isfield Church to Isfield Bridge. There is a single Type 24 pillbox (A238) near the motte and bailey south of Isfield Church (TQ 4435 1803) and another built into the garden wall of Isfield Place (TQ446184) which has been disguised to match the buttresses on either side of it. To the south of Church Lane hidden in a small copse (TQ446184) is a Type 28 anti-tank pillbox covering Isfield Bridge.

54 Type 28A anti-tank pillbox (A243) located on a field boundary north of the Anchor Inn at Barcombe (TQ 4422 1644)

At Isfield Bridge itself, there are two Type 24 pillboxes. The first (A237) is to the south of the bridge and situated on the west side of, and facing towards, the road (TQ 4486 1814). The second (A234) is situated north of the bridge, along Church Lane to the rear of Bridge Cottage (TQ 4482 1820). This faces towards the bridge and has a brick chimney on the north-east corner of its roof (a surviving part of its camouflage), although this is now very overgrown and difficult to see. The bridge was probably prepared for demolition and must have originally had a roadblock, although the only indications of this are two discarded anti-tank buoys lying in the river on the west side of the bridge.

East of Isfield Bridge there are four Type 24 pillboxes following the river until it turns north and is crossed by the bridge of the disused railway line. From here the next few pillboxes are located along the railway line embankment until it re-crosses the river, after this the pillboxes are once again situated on the west and north bank of the river as it passes to the south of Uckfield.

At Buckham Hill, on the minor road from Isfield Bridge north towards Shortbridge, is evidence of a roadblock. A single coffin can be seen in the hedge on the east side of the road at TQ 4514 2070, whilst a parch mark between this and the road shows the position of another coffin, since removed. In a gateway on the opposite side of the road are the concrete bases of further coffins.

Isfield camp (TQ451171) was used as an industrial park for some years, but is now deserted and awaiting redevelopment. The camp at Maresfield is currently used as a training centre for the East Sussex Fire Brigade, and many of the original buildings have now been removed. However, the original guardhouse survives at TQ 4577 2365 and is currently used as a dining hall, and the cinema located in Uckfield High Street was originally built for the soldiers based at Maresfield Camp in 1916.

Directions and access

The two pillboxes near the Anchor Inn can be seen from the adjacent footpath or road. To see the Type 28A, walk north from Anchor Lane across public access land on the west side of the dismantled railway, where it can be seen at a field boundary west of the railway bridge. To find the pillboxes between here and Isfield, take the footpath from Anchor Lane to Blunts Lane. The first pillbox (A242) is on the footpath at TQ 4421 1683 and has a high step-up into the entrance with a drainage pipe through the concrete step. The second (A241) sits behind the Longford Stream at TQ 4424 1711 and has a similar entrance, suggesting that the drainage problems on this low-lying land were recognised by the builders. The next two pillboxes (A240 and A239) are both on private land (at TQ 4421 1768 and TQ 4412 1747 respectively) to the west of the footpath.

There is a small lay-by south of Isfield Bridge and Mill. The first Type 24 pillbox (A237) is on private farmland immediately beside the adjacent field entrance. Cross the bridge and turn into Church Lane where the pillbox with the chimney is located behind Bridge Cottages. The pillbox incorporated into the wall of

Isfield Place can be seen through the hedge to the north of Church Lane, whilst the Type 28 pillbox can be seen to the south. The Type 24 pillbox south of Isfield Church can be seen across the field from the church car park. All of these are on private land.

A footpath east of Isfield Place can be followed to the railway bridge over the River Uck. The first two pillboxes here are well hidden and could not be seen on a summer visit; furthermore, they are both situated on private land. The two that can be seen from the adjacent footpath are A233, which is situated on a hedge line overlooking the bend in the River Uck at TQ 4547 1829 and to its rear, on the north side of the footpath, hidden in the undergrowth is A227 (TQ 4546 1834).

To find the roadblock at Buckham Hill, follow the minor road north from Isfield Bridge. The coffin can be seen in the hedge on the right just before the road junction.

SITE 35: BUXTED

Period:	**Second World War**
Type of site:	**Pillboxes**

History

After Uckfield the GHQ Stop Line follows the River Uck north to Buxted, and then on to Howbourne Farm, just to the north of Buxted. The River Uck then heads east towards Mayfield and its source, whilst the Stop Line heads northwards to follow the line of the railway towards Crowborough.

The main concentration of defences at Buxted was located close to the road bridge over the River Uck at Buxted Park. Here two Type 24 pillboxes and two machine gun emplacements were located to the north and south of the road covering the bridge, whilst a further pillbox was situated a little further west along the road to provide defence in depth. One kilometre further west along the A272 road, two Type 24 pillboxes covered Lepham's Bridge.

Following the River Uck north from Buxted through to Howbourne Farm are more pillboxes, after which they begin to follow the line of the railway, with a dozen pillboxes on the high ground through to Burnt Oak and Fordbrook. There were also a number of pillboxes built to cover road bridges on minor roads to the west of the main Stop Line.

The sites today

At Buxted Park an unusual machine gun emplacement survives at TQ 4915 2320. It comprises a rectangular brick-shuttered concrete emplacement with chamfered corners and a chamfered edge to the concrete roof (55). The entrance is on its north side and it has two embrasures facing east towards the river, with single embrasures in the south and west walls. Also in the park is the concrete base of a demolished pillbox adjacent to the A272 road (TQ 4902 2332). A Type 24 pillbox (A190?) is located in the grounds of Buxted Lodge (TQ 4928 2325) facing the bridge. On the north side of the road, on the edge of Parsonage Wood, are a second Type 24 and another machine gun emplacement.

In Buxted village are two wooden sectional huts – possible survivors from a small military camp located here (TQ 4975 2324). The first hut is used by the 1st Buxted Scout Group, while the second, located a little to the north, is used for agricultural purposes and has an added breezeblock extension. Another wooden building and an overgrown brick building nearby may also be survivors from the same camp.

The first of the Type 24 pillboxes covering Lepham's Bridge is situated on slightly higher ground, close to the road, on the south-west side of the bridge and facing east (TQ 4816 2357). The second is located to the north of the bridge, on the high ground adjacent to Lepham's Bridge House, facing south (TQ 4823 2370). Other pillboxes are located to the north of Buxted covering minor roads to the rear of the Stop Line. The first (A177) is near the Hermitage (TQ493250), south of High Hurstwood, and the second is situated on a bank beside Burnt Oak Lane, near Burnt Oak (TQ 5112 2698). This latter pillbox (A164) is a thin-walled Type 24 pillbox with small embrasures and sits on a large concrete base on the south side of the lane.

55 The machine gun emplacement at Buxted Park (TQ 4915 2320). The entrance is on its north side, with the two embrasures shown facing east towards the river

North of Buxted, at Huggett's Farm, is a Type 24 pillbox (A180) at TQ 5037 2478. This faces south-east covering a track and footbridge over the Uck. Two further pillboxes (A178 and A179) are located to the south of the railway embankment, overlooking the river, near Foxhole Farm, and then at Howbourne Farm is another group of pillboxes. The most interesting of these sits on the north bank of the river at TQ 5128 2506, just to the west of Howbourne Farm, and retains its original camouflage (*colour plate 20*). It is a standard Type 24 pillbox (A175) but has a pitched roof constructed from wire mesh and a thin layer of concrete to make it look like a small building. Two further Type 24s are located to the north of the farm; the first (A174) sits in the centre of a field facing east at TQ 5140 2518, whilst the second (A173?) is located further uphill in a hedge line at TQ 5116 2539, also facing east.

East of the farm and situated in a hedge line at TQ 5158 2537 is a 'squashed' Type 24 pillbox, which originally covered a small bridge across the River Uck to its south. It has an external brick blast wall with two pistol ports, but no internal blast wall. The bridge has now gone, but a single coffin survives on the south bank of the river to mark its location (TQ 5163 2533); a second coffin appears to have now fallen into the river.

To the east of the railway line as it heads northwards are further Type 24 pillboxes placed at regular intervals. At Fordbrook there were four pillboxes covering the road junction and bridge, including a Type 28 anti-tank pillbox. At Sparrow Cottages (TQ 5239 2716) is a thick-walled Type 24 pillbox (A155) facing south across the valley, covering a track and protecting the rear of another similar Type 24 (A156), which is located a little further south on a bank beside the track. Both of these pillboxes are similar, with in situ wooden frames surviving in two embrasures of the pillbox at Sparrow Cottages.

Directions and access

All of the sites mentioned are on private property and cannot be viewed without permission, except for the following examples: the Type 24 pillbox covering Lepham's Bridge from the west can be seen from the A272 road, with a lay-by situated about 100m past the bridge for parking. A footpath runs south from Buxted Lodge right past the machine gun emplacement in Buxted Park. The sectional hut is located beside a small green off Framfield Road in Buxted. The pillbox in Burnt Oak Lane is beside the road, but difficult to see due to the vegetation.

The Pillbox at Huggett's Farm can also be visited as it is on the Vanguard Way, south of Fowly Lane. Continuing east along Fowly Lane another footpath takes you south, across the railway line and on to Howbourne Farm. Pillboxes A173 and A174 are situated adjacent to the footpath, but the other sites here cannot be visited, although the camouflaged pillbox can be seen in the distance through a field entrance to the west of the footpath. The pillboxes at Sparrow Cottages can be seen from the adjacent track, although they are both on private property.

SITE 36: CROWBOROUGH

Period: **Second World War**
Type of site: **Pillboxes**

History

Jarvis Brook to the east of Crowborough was designated as a Nodal Point due to its location on the GHQ Stop Line and also because Crowborough railway station and an important road junction were located there. Additionally, it protected the eastern approach into Crowborough itself. The pillboxes that had been following the GHQ Stop Line along the railway northwards from Buxted continued around Jarvis Brook and then followed the railway again northwards to Groombridge, supplemented by an anti-tank ditch in places. The main road from Rotherfield to Crowborough (B2100) was blocked at Maynards Gate by a roadblock, which was covered by a Type 28 anti-tank pillbox, with another pillbox immediately to its rear. Pillboxes also covered the southern approaches by road and railway into Jarvis Brook.

The eastern approach to Crowborough town was protected by a pair of pillboxes on the B2100 at Crowborough Hill, whilst the main southern approach (A26 road) had pillboxes at Heron's Ghyll and Newnham Park Farm. Crowborough was provided with both public and private air-raid shelters, whilst others were built at schools in the town.

Later in the war the railway station and marshalling yard at Jarvis Brook were the delivery point for tanks arriving by train for training exercises in Ashdown Forest. The road (Crowborough Hill) leading from the station through Crowborough was concreted and camps were constructed to the west of the town to accommodate the soldiers.

The sites today

The first of a number of local 'Crowborough' type pillboxes can be found guarding the southern approach into Crowborough from Hadlow Down at TQ 5305 2881. It comprises a square brick-built pillbox with pre-cast concrete embrasures in its south and west walls, and is located in a raised position on a bank beside the road (56). The railway cutting and bridge south of Jarvis Brook is covered by a Type 24 pillbox (A139) situated in the grounds of the Baptist Church in Walshes Road (TQ 5296 2918). A second pillbox may have been located nearby at TQ530292, but there is no trace of this today. Two 'Crowborough' type pillboxes on Crowborough Hill were partly sunken into the ground in the gardens of houses covering the road junction with Green Lane and Tollwood Road. Built with 8.5in-thick brick walls and concrete roofs, both pillboxes had steps down to the entrance with pre-cast concrete embrasures covering the road junction. The pillbox in Holly Lodge was partly demolished during road junction improvements and the pillbox in Cob Cottage has also been partly demolished at some stage in the past.

56 A Crowborough Type pillbox in a raised position on a bank beside the road guarding the southern approach into Crowborough from Hadlow Down at TQ 5305 2881

Crowborough Training Camp (TQ 497298) continues in use today, along with the adjacent training area of Pippingford Park. A second camp (West Camp) was initially tented, but later had permanent buildings. Some of these buildings are now used as a hospital and the camp is no longer used by the military. The brick-built guardhouse and entrance gate to West Camp can be seen at TQ 5022 3202, off the minor road from the town centre to Marden's Hill.

To the south-east of Jarvis Brook, a Type 28 and a Type 24 are located alongside the drive to Rotherfield Hall off Trebler's Road and face south to cover this approach into the Nodal Point. Two more Type 24s continue the GHQ Stop Line north to the B2100 at Maynards Gate where a bridge crosses the stream. A Type 28, with a holdfast for a Hotchkiss 6pdr gun, is situated at the entrance to the Jarvis Brook Depot (TQ 5410 2973) and covers the bridge, whilst its adjacent pillbox has either been demolished or covered over. Although nothing survives of the roadblock that was situated here, seven pimples can be seen blocking the bridleway to the south of the bridge (TQ 5417 2969), where the anti-tank ditch met the sunken track.

The GHQ Stop Line now follows the railway north through Old Lodge Warren, where some 13 pillboxes survive. Most of these are standard Type 24 pillboxes, but there are a number of variants, together with two further examples of the local 'Crowborough' variant pillbox. The first pillbox (A121) is situated at TQ 542299 to the north of the ford along Palesgate Road, where it was located behind the anti-tank ditch which continued north to the next Type 24 (A118) at TQ 542302. Entering the Woodland Trust land the next Type 24 (A117) is situated at the top of the steep stream bank at TQ 5414 3020. A little further along and partly sunk into the railway embankment on the north-west side of the track is a 'Crowborough' type pillbox, with a single pre-cast embrasure facing south-east (TQ 5421 3029). It is difficult to find, but has a protected passage with steps down to its entrance, and the concrete roof is partly dislodged. Next is an unusual Type 24 variant (TQ 5427 3040) that has been built on a thick concrete base at the bottom of the railway embankment. It has a thick extended rear wall, with its entrance in the north wall; there is no internal blast wall and it only has four embrasures.

The next six Type 24 pillboxes are all located at the top of the stream bank. A114 (TQ 5444 3061) is some way south of the track and difficult to locate. A113 (TQ 5458 3088) has extensive blast damage, which has exposed the reinforced concrete construction and A112 (TQ 5459 3097) covers a path to a ford across the stream. A111 is set into the stream bank at TQ 5471 3119 and has seven brick-edged steps down to its entrance (57). A110 covers a footbridge across the stream close to a disused pumping station at TQ 5473 3136 and has an entrance passage with steps and a low retaining wall to its entrance. Its concrete base is badly undermined by erosion caused by the stream (*colour plate 21*). A109 (TQ 5480 3155) is terraced into the top of the stream bank, with a minor stream on its west side, and uses a deeper red-coloured brick.

The final Type 24 pillbox (A108) also has the deeper red-coloured bricks and is terraced into the slope facing east at TQ 5496 3180. At the north end of the woodland a surviving section of a machine-cut anti-tank ditch can be seen, although now very overgrown. It approaches from the south and turns to the north-east, at which point there is a 'Crowborough' Type pillbox partly sunk into the ground at TQ 5500 3187. This pillbox has two pre-cast embrasures, one each in the south and east walls, covering the anti-tank ditch.

Directions and access

The 'Crowborough' Type pillbox situated on the Hadlow Down to Crowborough road has a small lay-by beside it and is the most accessible example of this type. Other pillboxes to the south of Jarvis Brook and those on Crowborough Hill are on private land and cannot be visited. To visit the pillboxes at Maynards Gate and Old Lodge Warren, it is best to park along Palesgate Road, where there are some spaces to the north of the ford. Walk back to the B2100 to see the Type 28 in the entrance to Jarvis Brook Depot and the pimples along the bridleway. Access to Old Lodge Warren is via a stile beside the railway line in Palesgate Road. The first two Type 24 pillboxes in Old Lodge Warren are on private land and cannot be visited, but once you enter the Woodland Trust land all are accessible. Follow the track through Hornshurst Wood between the stream and the railway line, most are situated close to the path and easy to find – although A114 to A112 are more difficult to locate – but by following minor paths on the right of the track they

57 Type 24 pillbox A111 is set into the stream bank at TQ 5471 3119 in Old Lodge Warren, and has seven brick-edged steps down to its entrance

can be found beside the stream. It is worth remembering that this area was much more open at the time the pillboxes were constructed.

References/Background reading

Foot, W. 2006a, *Beaches, fields, streets and hills: the anti-invasion landscapes of England*, CBA Research Report 144, York, Council for British Archaeology

Foot, W. 2006b, *The Battlefields That Nearly Were*, Stroud, Tempus Publishing Ltd

SITE 37: ERIDGE

Period:	**Second World War**
Type of site:	**Pillboxes**

History

The pillboxes followed the GHQ Stop Line along the railway north to Eridge Station, where they then headed north-west, still on the west side of the railway line to Groombridge, where the Stop Line picked up the River Medway. The pillboxes on this section of the GHQ Stop Line were predominantly brick-shuttered Type 24, but from Eridge Station northwards most are wood-shuttered. These were supplemented by Type 28 anti-tank pillboxes, which covered bridges and other vulnerable points.

The sites today

Just to the north of Old Lodge Warren two railway lines meet, with bridges carrying the lines over the road. A Type 24 pillbox (A106) sits on the bank beside the road opposite Redgate Mill Farm facing north-east along the road (TQ 5526 3239). Although this is a standard Type 24 pillbox, it is of interest because the concrete lintel above the entrance has some wartime graffiti comprising a man's head with a crown above it and the words 'The Kings Head' below it. Another Type 24 pillbox is situated to the rear of Mead Farm on the north-west side of the bridges (TQ550326).

At Copyhold Farm there is a Type 28 pillbox sitting alongside the farm buildings (TQ 5433 3388), facing north-east to cover the railway/road bridge. It has a single embrasure for the anti-tank gun and two smaller embrasures in the side walls, with a large entrance in the rear wall. Unusually for a Type 28 on this Stop Line, its number (A100) survives on the right side of the entrance. A single Type 24 sits in the centre of a field north of Sandhill Farm (approximately TQ546334), whilst at Hamsell Farm there are two Type 24 pillboxes covering the railway line as it approaches Eridge Station. The first (A98) is near the farm buildings (TQ 5441 3424) and faces east, whilst the second (A97) is on the east side of the railway embankment (TQ 5445 3435) facing south-east. North of Eridge Station is a Type 24 pillbox (A90), between the railway line and the road (TQ539347), with the next group located in Ligg Wood. A partly sunken Type 24 pillbox (A88) with an L-shaped porch and steps to its entrance is situated on the wooded slope (TQ 5345 3488), whilst on the south-east edge of the wood is a sunken 'Crowborough' Type pillbox that has partly collapsed (TQ 5344 3483). At the north end of Ligg Wood is another Type 24 pillbox (approximately TQ533350), also situated on the wooded slope.

The next Type 24 (A85) is a little further north and located on the top of the roadside bank (TQ 5315 3519). This is the first of the wood-shuttered pillboxes, and is partly sunk into the slope and facing north to cover the bridges across the railway and river to Forge Farm. As the railway curves round to the north, another Type 24 (A83) is positioned in a field boundary, facing north-east (TQ530354).

To the south of Groombridge there is a group of four pillboxes between the two diverging railway lines, covering the road bridge over the river to the north. A partly sunken Type 24 facing east sits in a field opposite the cemetery at TQ530362, with another Type 24 in the wooded edge of the cemetery (TQ 5295 3625), facing north-east. A Type 28 pillbox facing north sits in a private garden to the east of the road (TQ530363) and has a modern structure on its roof. The final Type 24 is in the open ground, behind a small stream (TQ 5284 3638), and faces north to the bridge.

Continuing westwards there are more Type 24 pillboxes covering the river and small farm access tunnels under the railway embankment. Four Type 24 pillboxes sit in the same field (58), with two situated forward close to the river (TQ 5265 3636 and near Sherlock's Wood TQ 5233 3635) and two built into the slope further

58 Two of the four Type 24 pillboxes situated in the same field south of Groombridge. The pillbox in the foreground (TQ 5273 3628) has its entrance in the nearest side wall and only four embrasures, covering the pillbox to its front and tunnels under the railway embankment

back to provide defence in depth (TQ 5242 3610 and TQ 5273 3628). The last of these is unusual, in that it has its entrance in the east side wall; it has a standard internal blast wall, but only four embrasures. North of Alksford Farm there are two Type 24 pillboxes, one in the corner of a garden, one beside Sherlock's Wood (TQ523364), the second set into a slope in the middle of a field (TQ 5212 3634). Both of these face north to cover Hendal Bridge, along with two further Type 24 pillboxes located at Hendal Farm (TQ 518364 and TQ519364).

Directions and access

Many of the pillboxes on this section of the Stop Line are on private property, although some can easily be seen from adjacent roads and footpaths. The Type 28 at Copyhold Farm can be seen from the adjacent footpath that passes through the farm from the A26 road, but those at Hamsell Farm are not accessible. The pillboxes at Ligg Wood and further along the lane near Forge Farm can be seen from the lane in winter. Some of the pillboxes south of Groombridge can be visited by parking near the cemetery and following the footpath west from the road opposite the tennis courts. Pass the first pillbox and then follow the footpath under the railway embankment to find the four pillboxes in the same field. None of the pillboxes at Hendal Bridge can be visited.

SITE 38: WITHYHAM

Period: **Second World War**
Type of site: **Pillboxes**

History

From Groombridge the GHQ Stop Line followed the River Medway up to the Kent border. Although the river became the main anti-tank barrier for the Stop Line, the railway line continued to follow a parallel route alongside the river, forming an additional barrier on its east side. A number of pillboxes were also located to the rear of the Stop Line, especially along the B2110 road to Hartfield, where a group of pillboxes were clustered around the roadblock at Hewkins Bridge, near Withyham.

The sites today

Many of the pillboxes survive along this part of the line from Groombridge northwards to the Kent border. At Ham Bridge on the B2110 road, there are three Type 24 pillboxes and a single Type 28 covering the bridge. The first Type 24 is situated alongside the road at TQ 5128 3678 in a sunken position within the hedgerow facing along the road. To the east of the road is a second Type 24 (A59) in the corner of Hendal Wood (TQ 5143 3673) and a short distance further south is a Type 28 (TQ 5137 3670). This is brick shuttered with an embrasure with a 6pdr holdfast (59) facing north, an internal blast wall and a single small embrasure in the west wall, together with a large entrance in the rear wall. The final Type 24 (A55) is on the west of the road near the disused railway and occupies a sunken position beside the river (TQ 5129 3693). Further west along the disused railway there is a Type 24 partly sunk into the top of the embankment of a cutting (TQ 5102 3698), and a little further beyond this a Type 28 sits on the top of the railway embankment facing east (TQ 5098 3696). This has a single embrasure with a 6pdr holdfast, an internal blast wall and two small embrasures in the side walls, with a large entrance in the rear wall.

Type 24 pillboxes then follow the river north. A50 sits in the middle of a field to the north of the disused railway (TQ 5108 3708) and A49 is in a small copse (TQ 5107 3737) covering the bridge and track between Ham Farm and Hale Court Farm. Three pillboxes continue the line north to Ashurst Bridge, where two more are located in semi-sunken positions along a hedgeline (TQ 5067 3817 and TQ 5045 3835) set back from the river and a third sits further forward in the centre of the field (TQ 5055 3856).

At Ashurst Bridge there are two Type 24 pillboxes on the south side of the road covering the bridge; the first sits on a large concrete base beside the road (TQ 5044 3893), whilst the second is partly sunken a short distance further south (TQ 5047 3888). North of the bridge is a Type 28 pillbox, very overgrown and in a sunken location with a large rear entrance (TQ 5051 3902), and a

59 The 6pdr holdfast in the Type 28 anti-tank pillbox at Hendal Wood (TQ 5137 3670), covering Ham Bridge near Withyham

little further north there is a Type 24 sitting on an island (TQ 5051 3907), both covering the bridge from this direction. The railway bridge crosses the river a little further north and is covered by a Type 24 pillbox in the edge of a wood (TQ 5052 3919).

Further north a group of three Type 24 pillboxes is located around a copse between the river and the railway. The first (A34) is on low ground close to the river (TQ 5058 3943), and faces south to cover the river and open ground between the river and railway. The second (A35) sits in a sunken position on higher ground on the west edge of the copse (TQ 5055 3942) and faces south, covering the open ground and a farm tunnel under the railway embankment. The final pillbox (A32) is on the north edge of the copse (TQ 5060 3950) and faces east towards the river. Two further Type 24s located on the low ground to the east of Willett's Farm complete the Sussex part of the GHQ Stop Line.

Along the B2110 to the rear of the Stop Line is an unusual two-storey pillbox at View House (TQ 5083 3653). It resembles a Type 24, having an entrance at ground floor level, but no embrasures. There are steps up to the first floor at one side, with an internal blast wall and four embrasures in the remaining short walls, and with two smaller embrasures in the long rear wall.

At Hewkins Bridge at Withyham, on the B2110 road, there are four anti-tank pimples remaining from the roadblock that was sited here (TQ 4926 3568) and covering the bridge are three pillboxes. The first (A73) is beside the road in a sunken position facing the bridge (TQ 4919 3569), with the second (A72) partly

60 Thin-walled Type 24 pillbox A71 terraced into the slope on the north side of the road facing Hewkins Bridge, Withyham TQ 4916 3577

sunk into the slope of the hill (TQ 4909 3575) protecting its rear. Both of these are standard wood-shuttered thick-walled Type 24 pillboxes. The third pillbox (A71) is terraced into the slope on the north side of the road facing the bridge (TQ 4916 3577) and is a thin-walled Type 24 with five small embrasures (*60*).

Directions and access

At Ham Bridge, park near the bridge, and follow the footpath west along the disused railway track to see the Type 24 and Type 28 pillboxes at the railway cutting. Two other Type 24 pillboxes can be seen by taking the footpath (Wealdway) north from the disused railway. The pillboxes on the east side of the road are on private land, but the one beside the road can be seen in the hedge. Taking the B2110 west to Hartfield, you will pass the two-storey pillbox at View House, then passing through Withyham, park near Hewkins Bridge to see the anti-tank pimples. The two thick-walled pillboxes are adjacent to the footpath west of the bridge, so can be visited.

Park in the lay-by at Ashurst Bridge to visit the pillboxes here. The first two are immediately beside the footpath to the south of the lay-by. To see those further south, walk along the A264 under the railway bridge to find the footpath that takes you back across the weir and then along the west bank of the river. Return to the lay-by and cross the road following the footpath north. The overgrown

Type 28 and a Type 24 can be seen beyond the stream on the right, but there is no access to them. Before you reach the railway bridge the next Type 24 is on the edge of the wood across the field. Pass under the railway bridge, following the footpath to find the Type 24 in the copse beside the river; the other two pillboxes can be found on the north and west sides of the copse. The pillboxes at Willett's Farm cannot be visited.

References/Background reading

Martin, R.G. 2002, *Pillbox at View House*, Withyham, Unpublished

4

INLAND DEFENCE SITES
IN EAST SUSSEX

This final chapter covers all of the inland sites not already covered in the previous chapters. These range in date from the Napoleonic barracks at Ringmer and Iden Lock on the Royal Military Canal, through to the Second World War and the Cold War, although the majority of the sites that remain to be seen date from the Second World War. These include the Corps Stop Line that follows the River Ouse westwards and the pillboxes along the Rivers Uck and Rother to the east. There are also two airfields, at Chailey and Deanland, together with a number of Nodal Points and the important radar sites at Wartling and Pevensey Levels. Cold War sites include ROC posts, bunkers and depot sites.

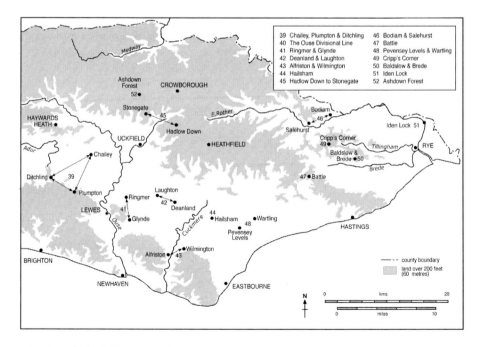

39 Chailey, Plumpton & Ditchling	46 Bodiam & Salehurst
40 The Ouse Divisional Line	47 Battle
41 Ringmer & Glynde	48 Pevensey Levels & Wartling
42 Deanland & Laughton	49 Cripp's Corner
43 Alfriston & Wilmington	50 Baldslow & Brede
44 Hailsham	51 Iden Lock
45 Hadlow Down to Stonegate	52 Ashdown Forest

61 Map of inland sites in East Sussex

SITE 39: CHAILEY, PLUMPTON AND DITCHLING

Period: **Second World War and Cold War**
Type of site: **Advanced Landing Ground, tank road and ROC post**

History

The proposed Chailey ALG was surveyed in 1942 and the land requisitioned in January 1943. Construction started soon afterwards, which involved the felling of many trees and the removal of the Plough Inn to its current site. Two runways were laid out approximately north–south and east–west using Sommerfield Track, together with areas of hardstanding and a fuel dump. Four Over Blister hangars were erected, but apart from the requisitioned Bower Farmhouse and Westlands Cottages, which were used as headquarters, all other accommodation was under canvas. The airfield was defended by four 40mm Bofors and sixteen 20mm Hispano guns of No. 2882 Squadron RAF Regiment.

In April No. 131 Airfield arrived from Deanland ALG (Site 42) with its three Polish squadrons and was soon operating fighter-bomber missions over France. Renamed 131 Wing, they provided cover for the D-Day landings before moving to Appledram ALG on 28 June. Chailey ALG was put under Care and Maintenance, and it was retained as an emergency airfield until de-requisitioned in January 1945.

Plumpton Agricultural College was used during the Second World War to train Land Army personnel and large areas of Downland nearby were used as army training areas. To enable tanks and other vehicles to access the training areas, concrete roads were constructed, often using existing trackways such the Plumpton Bostall.

Lodge Hill, Ditchling, was the site of an ROC underground Monitoring Post, which opened in June 1962 and was closed in November 1970.

The sites today

After de-requisition, Chailey airfield was cleared and quickly reverted to agricultural purposes, the only clues today being the hedgeless landscape where the runways were located and the brick pumphouse building (62) on the site of the bulk fuel installation (TQ 3685 1889). The requisitioned farmhouse and cottages are still present, and a metalled track and other remains of the domestic site can be found in Plumpton Wood. Some of the Sommerfield Track removed from the airfield apparently survives at Plumpton Racecourse.

On 5th August 2000 an air display was held on the site of the ALG, which attracted thousands of visitors, and a memorial at the Plough Inn (TQ 3652 1817) was dedicated to those who had served at Chailey ALG.

Around the Ditchling and Plumpton area there are many anti-tank buoys marking the entrances to farms and other properties. Examples can be found at 'Shirleys', Ditchling (TQ 3331 1487), Stocks Farm, Spatham Lane (TQ 3385 1602), Home Farm, Slugwash lane (TQ 3529 2211), 'Bathfield', St Helena's Lane

62 The brick pumphouse building on the site of the bulk fuel installation at Chailey ALG adjacent to Beresford Lane (TQ 3685 1889)

(TQ 3621 1811) and at Plumpton Agricultural College (TQ 3584 1340) where some 20 line the driveway.

The Plumpton Bostall tank road (TQ 3636 1317) starts on a sharp corner of the B2116, opposite the Half Moon public house, and climbs up to Plumpton Plain. Its central section retains the original concrete surface, including grooves to assist traction on the steep slope. Further up the concrete surface has deteriorated, but the brick rubble hardcore that formed the base for the road can be seen.

The ROC monitoring post on Lodge Hill, Ditchling is still extant and some of its above-ground features still survive (TQ 3234 1563). A metal handrail and dismantled steps from Lodge Hill Lane up to a locked gate indicate the original entrance to the post. A modern lid has sealed the access hatch, but the original air vent is still present.

Directions and access

Chailey ALG can be found by taking North Common Lane south from the A272 at North Chailey and then turning into Beresford Lane towards Plumpton. The runways of the ALG crossed Beresford Lane at TQ371 193. A little further along Beresford Lane on its west side is the site of the bulk fuel installation. The brick pumphouse can be seen from the footpath that starts in Beresford Lane and crosses the east-west runway.

For the tank road, there is a small lay-by in Plumpton Lane; from here cross the B2116 with care and follow the footpath opposite.

To find the ROC monitoring post at Ditchling, park at the pond beside the churchyard off the B2116 to Keymer. Walk north along Lodge Hill Lane and past the dismantled steps to the site. A short distance further on is a gate and stile on the right with permitted access onto Lodge Hill.

References/Background reading

Ashworth, R.C.B. 1985, *Action Stations 9. Military airfields of the Central South and South-East*, Wellingborough, Patrick Stephens Ltd

Brooks, R.J. 1993, *Sussex Airfields in the Second World War*, Newbury, Countryside Books

Whittle, R. 2004, *Spit & Polish*, Boxer Productions

www.subbrit.org.uk/cgi-bin/webdata_roc.pl

SITE 40: GUILDFORD TO UCKFIELD CORPS STOP LINE

Period: **Second World War**
Type of site: **Pillboxes**

History

The main GHQ Stop Line ran north through Sussex from Newhaven to the Kent border. However, this was not the only Stop Line in Sussex, as a Corps Stop Line continued to follow the line of the River Ouse west from Uckfield through into West Sussex and then on to Guildford in Surrey. This line was not as strongly protected as the GHQ Stop Line, as its defences were concentrated at the bridges over the River Ouse. Each bridge was provided with anti-tank coffins and other blocks such as cylinders and buoys, whilst Type 28 anti-tank pillboxes and Type 24 pillboxes, usually one of each type at each bridge, were constructed to defend these crossing points. The River Ouse was modified to improve its ability to act as an anti-tank ditch by cutting the north bank vertically and revetting it with timber.

The sites today

Many of the pillboxes covering the bridges still survive, although some have been removed. However, few of the coffins or other blocks remain as they have been removed as a result of road and bridge widening schemes since the war.

At Sharpsbridge there is a single coffin (*63*) remaining on the north-west side of Sharp's Bridge (TQ 4395 2076), whilst a short distance to the north-west is a Type 28A pillbox (TQ 4385 2075). This pillbox sits in a field and has a holdfast for a 6pdr Hotchkiss facing the bridge. It has an external L-shaped blast wall protecting the entrance, which unusually enters the machine gun compartment in a side wall. It is possible that there was a Type 24 pillbox also covering the bridge, but there is no trace of this today.

63 The coffin at Sharp's Bridge (TQ 4395 2076) with its adjacent Type 28A pillbox covering the bridge from the field behind

A Type 28A pillbox covers Gold Bridge to the east of Newick, where the A272 crosses the River Ouse. A Type 24 pillbox was positioned at approximately TQ 430214, but has been removed. The pillbox sits in the corner of a field to the north-east of the bridge (TQ 4282 2161) and contains a holdfast for a 6pdr Hotchkiss. The bridge is modern and no trace of any roadblock survives.

At Fletching Mill Bridges a Type 28A variant pillbox, with a machine gun compartment located on either side of the anti-tank gun compartment, covers the bridge from the east (TQ427228). A Type 24 pillbox is situated alongside the road to Fletching (TQ 4255 2307) and has an external blast wall, though no embrasure in its east wall. There is no surviving evidence for any roadblock at the two bridges here.

A single Type 24 pillbox with an external blast wall is situated to the east of Sheffield Bridge (TQ 4070 2354), near Sheffield Park railway station. A second pillbox may have been located to the north-west of the station, perhaps covering the railway bridge over the River Ouse.

Directions and access

Sharp's Bridge can be found by taking the minor road to Shortbridge from the A272 at Piltdown, then turning right opposite Piltdown Pond. Parking is difficult at the bridge and the Type 28A pillbox is on private farmland. Return to Piltdown and turn left onto the A272 towards Newick, after 1.5km there is a lay-by adjacent to Gold Bridge. The type 28A pillbox can be seen to the north of the bridge, but is on private

farmland. Continue into Newick and take a minor road north to Fletching Common,
turning right to Fletching after 1km. This takes you to Fletching Mill Bridges, where
there is a pull-in on the right after the bridges. The Type 28A is difficult to see in
the field boundary to the east of the bridges, and there is no public access to it. A
little further on pull in at the entrance to the sewage works to find the adjacent
well-hidden Type 24 beside the road. Follow the road north through Fletching and
round to Sheffield Park, turning south onto the A275. At Sheffield Bridge go to the
overflow car park for the Bluebell Railway on the left before the bridge. The Type 24
pillbox is situated in the corner of the field on the far side of the car park.

SITE 41: RINGMER AND GLYNDE

Period: **Napoleonic to Cold War**
Type of site: **Barracks, radio masts, trenches and depot**

History

An artillery barracks was built at Ringmer in 1795 to house 276 men and 92
horses. It comprised accommodation for officers and men, stables, a hospital and
a magazine. With the end of the Napoleonic Wars, the site became surplus to
requirements and was sold off in 1827-8.

   During the Second World War The Caburn (TQ444089) appears to have been
put into a state of defence, with a number of slit trenches dug within the ramparts
of the Iron Age hillfort, suggesting a platoon position. Anti-aircraft guns were also
possibly positioned on The Caburn. A railway gun was positioned in the chalk pit at
Glynde (TQ460086) and was apparently painted white to assist in its camouflage.

   Beddingham Hill is dominated today by two radio masts and their associated
buildings (TQ 4579 0591). Within the security compound are the concrete bases
and anchors for earlier masts, although it is not clear whether these had any
military function. Concrete tank roads were built to take tanks onto the Downs,
one running from Little Dene to Beddingham Hill and another from Firle. On
the top of Beddingham Hill are a series of small slit trenches and weapons pits
commanding the junction of footpaths and the tank road, perhaps a local defence
point or associated with training.

   During the Cold War numerous buffer storage depots were established across
the country to hold strategic reserves of food and other supplies for distribution
in the event of a nuclear attack or other emergency. One such depot, established
in 1948, was located to the north of Ringmer.

The sites today

After the barracks at Ringmer was sold off many of the original wooden buildings
were removed and new brick buildings added. The site is now used as kennels,
but a number of the original buildings survive. Fronting the B2124 is a large

timber-clad building (TQ 4609 1285), which may have originated as the officers accommodation whilst the large adjacent brick building also fronting the road was added in the 1870s. Set further back is a red and yellow brick building with a tiled roof (*colour plate 22*) that corresponds with the position of the hospital (TQ 4607 1278); the original well is still extant in an adjacent paddock. In the north-west corner of the site is a white-painted brick building with a slate roof, which may have been the original armoury (TQ 4600 1283), there being no trace of the associated magazine.

The Cold War buffer depot at Ringmer survives as The Caburn Enterprise Park (TQ 4630 1316). The guardroom and office is on the immediate left inside the entrance, with re-clad storage buildings (*64*) and Nissen huts arranged behind in two rows. Four anti-tank buoys can be found at the front of Ringmer Community College nearby (TQ 4547 1274).

Recent archaeological fieldwork on The Caburn has recorded the locations of a number of Second World War features, including slit trenches and possible anti-aircraft gun positions. In Glynde there is no trace of the railway gun position, but a concrete road leads into the chalk pit. Eight anti-tank buoys line the front gardens of properties in Lacys Hill in Glynde (TQ 4566 0910), whilst another seven buoys are incorporated into the hedge at the front entrance to Glyndbourne (TQ 4521 1066).

64 Storage units at the Cold War buffer depot at Ringmer, now re-clad and used as The Caburn Enterprise Park

On Beddingham Hill at least 10 trenches and weapons positions survive between TQ 4540 0609 and TQ 4544 0605. Although overgrown, the corrugated-iron linings retained by metal posts survive in most trenches, whilst to their rear is a larger L-shaped trench, perhaps the command trench.

Directions and access

The sites at Ringmer are situated at the north end of the village. The barracks are on the B2124 to Laughton, on the right immediately after the small roundabout. It is possible to park nearby and to view the buildings from the road. The buffer depot is on the B2192 to Uckfield on the right and signposted as The Caburn Enterprise Park. There is no parking here and the site is an industrial park with restricted access.

The Caburn can be reached by footpaths from Glynde or Lewes, whilst Beddingham Hill is best reached from the car park at the top of the old tank road from Firle. A short walk west from the car park brings you to the radio masts, with the trenches being a little further on, past the footpath junction.

References/Background reading

Drewett, P. and Hamilton, S. 1999, 'Marking time and making space', *Sussex Archaeological Collections* 137, 7-37

Elliston, R.A. 1999, *Lewes at War 1939-1945*, 2nd ed., Seaford, S.B. Publications

Goodwin, J.E. 2000, *Military Signals from the South Coast*, Midhurst, Middleton Press

Longstaff-Tyrrell, P. 2002, *Barracks to Bunkers*, Stroud, Sutton Publishing Ltd

SITE 42: DEANLAND AND LAUGHTON

Period: **Second World War**
Type of site: **Advanced Landing Ground and Observation Post**

History

Deanland was originally surveyed as a possible ALG in 1942, but it was not until July 1943 that work commenced with the arrival of No. 16 Airfield Construction Group RE. Two Summerfield Track runways were laid, orientated SE-NW and SW-NE, and later four Over Blister hangars were erected, together with four areas of concrete hardstanding as refuelling points. Local properties were requisitioned as officer's accommodation, with Broomham Farm becoming the Station HQ and Cleggets Farm an armoury and stores. Some Nissen huts were erected in Deanland Woods in 1944 as sleeping quarters.

No. 131 Airfield, comprising three squadrons formed from Polish personnel with Spitfires, were the first to move into Deanland on 1 April 1944, though they only stayed a short while before moving across to Chailey ALG (Site 39).

They were replaced by No.149 Airfield who operated three squadrons of Spitfires from Deanland in the period leading up to and throughout D-Day, before moving out by 26 June. On 21 July, two squadrons flying Spitfires arrived to help combat the V1 threat, being joined by a third squadron on 16 August. These squadrons left on 10 October 1944 and the airfield was officially closed in January 1945.

There are a number of other sites in the immediate area. At Chalvington, a short distance north of Deanland ALG, cropmarks on an aerial photograph showed a concentration of First World War practice trenches (TQ 5302 1197), whilst a number of buildings at Oakfield Farm nearby may be the remains of a military camp.

The sixteenth-century brick tower at Laughton Place is the only surviving structure within the moat (TQ 4835 1143). It was requisitioned as an observation post in the Second World War and had its timber roof removed and replaced with steel joists and a concrete top platform.

The sites today

Although part of the Deanland site is still used as an airfield, there is little to see of the ALG today, with most having reverted to agricultural purposes at the end of the war. A small area of concrete hardstanding from a refuelling point survives alongside Ripe Lane at TQ 5246 1139, with a second area and a section of road at TQ 5200 1136, adjacent to the entrance to Veals Farm. There are also reputedly remains of Nissen huts in Deanland Wood (c.TQ532117). A commemorative tree and plaque were placed near the current airfield buildings on 6 June 1994.

Laughton Tower is owned by the Landmark Trust and is now used for holiday letting.

Directions and access

Deanland ALG can be found by taking the minor road (Ripe Lane) from the A22 at Golden Cross towards Ripe. The surviving remains can be found between Deanland Park and the entrance to the airfield. There is no access to the airfield without prior arrangement.

Laughton Place can be reached by using one of a number of footpaths south of the B2124 (Laughton Road). There is no access to the Tower itself, but it can be viewed from the adjacent footpath.

References/Background reading

Ashworth, R.C.B. 1985, *Action Stations 9. Military airfields of the Central South and South-East*, Wellingborough, Patrick Stephens Ltd

Brooks, R.J. 1993, *Sussex Airfields in the Second World War*, Newbury, Countryside Books

Farrant, J., Howard, M., Rudling, D., Warren, J. and Whittick, C. 1991, 'Laughton Place: A Manorial and Architectural History with an account of recent restoration and excavation', *Sussex Archaeological Collections* 129, 99-164

Waring, P., Undated, *Deanland A.L.G. The History of a Sussex Airfield*, Laughton
   Air Museum

SITE 43: ALFRISTON AND WILMINGTON

Period: **Second World War**
Type of site: **Nodal Point, airfield and decoy site**

History

Alfriston sits on the west side of the River Cuckmere and occupies a strategic
position that could effectively block any advance along that side of the river
northwards from the coast; it was therefore designated as a Nodal Point in
1940. There were a number of defensive positions on the Alfriston Road from
Seaford, the first being a fixed flame defence situated at West Hill (approximately
TQ516016). This comprised a fuel tank located at the top of the bank on the east
side of the road, and a pipe leading from the tank down to the road at the bottom
of West Hill where it was pierced with holes. The fuel would have flowed down
the pipe by gravity onto the road where it would have been ignited.

   As the road enters Alfriston it turns sharply to the right and then sharply to
the left onto the High Street. Between these two bends was located a roadblock.
On the left of the road is a steep wooded slope, whilst on the opposite side was
the wall of Deans Place. The roadblock itself comprised removable anti-tank rails,
set into sockets in the road, and anti-tank buoys. The open flank of the roadblock
was protected by lines of anti-tank pimples, which followed the moated garden
feature in Deans Place and then crossed a ditch to continue down to the River
Cuckmere.

   To the north of Alfriston, Long Bridge (TQ 5243 0359), which provided the
first vehicle access across the River Cuckmere north of Exceat, was protected by
a roadblock and covered by a slit trench and a machine gun post. Interestingly,
there were no pillboxes constructed along the Cuckmere valley north of Exceat.

   A Starfish decoy site (SF79) was established at Alciston in November 1942 at
TQ504043 and also incorporated a QL site (QL91). These, together with the site
at Cuckmere Haven (Site 11), were used to simulate bombing attacks on Lewes
and Newhaven.

   Wilmington Airfield had been established as a Home Defence landing ground
in 1916 and had then been developed as an airfield during the 1930s with a
clubhouse, hangar and other buildings. It became the residence for the Sussex
Aero Club and although it was suggested that it should become the municipal
airport for Eastbourne, this came to nothing. The Eastbourne Flying Club was
established at the airfield in 1935 and a new Art Deco clubhouse was built in 1937.
An air show in 1938 attracted 10,000 spectators and 100 aircraft, including RAF
Gauntlets and a German Messerschmitt. When war broke out in 1939, the airfield

65 Some of the anti-tank pimples in Deans Place, Alfriston. The lines of pimples located here protected the open flank between the road block and the river

was closed and the runway blocked with cars. Two pillboxes were built to cover the runway, as although the airfield was never used during the war, there was a concern that the Germans would attempt to capture and use it in the event of an invasion.

The sites today

The fixed flame defence south of Alfriston was cleared away after the war and there is no trace of it at West Hill today. There is also no trace of the hairpin roadblock at the south end of the village, although some 18 anti-tank pimples survive in Deans Place (TQ 5198 0288-TQ 5202 0286) (65). The line of pimples crosses the ditch on the east side of Deans Place, where an anti-tank rail blocks access along the ditch. Another dozen pimples then continue the line towards the river. There is no trace of the slit trench or machine gun post at Long Bridge, but some 11 anti-tank buoys line the edge of the South Downs Way track at the nearby junction with the road to Milton Street (TQ 5257 0351). On the playing field lining North Road and The Furlongs in Alfriston are 116 anti-tank buoys (TQ517033). There is also a single dragon's tooth at the corner of the two roads. These buoys probably came from a number of different locations around the village, including the Deans Place roadblock.

The decoy site at Alciston was quickly removed at the end of the war. However, the overgrown remains of the partly demolished brick and concrete control shelter can be found at TQ 5038 0521.

The site of Wilmington Airfield has reverted to farmland and the clubhouse was demolished in the 1970s. The hangar remains on the site (TQ 5385 0509)

66 A thin-walled Type 24 pillbox facing across the runway now stands in a field boundary on the north-west side of Wilmington airfield (TQ 5362 0542)

and is currently used for agricultural purposes. A thin-walled Type 24 pillbox (66) stands on the north-west side of the airfield facing across the runway to the south (TQ 5362 0542). It has five small embrasures and the concrete roof has some corrugated-asbestos sheeting, which was used as shuttering, still in situ.

Directions and access
Deans Place is now a hotel and is located at the south end of the High Street. The pimples between Deans Place and the river can be seen to the right of the path from the road to the Clergy House. The pimples within the grounds of Deans Place are accessible to patrons of the hotel.

The playing field can be found by turning into West Street from the Market Cross on the High Street and then turning left into North Road. The playing field is just past the school on the left side of the road. Long Bridge is located to the north of the village, along North Street and down the right-hand turn signposted to Litlington.

To find the remains of the Alciston decoy site, turn into Alciston from the A27, and park near the church. Walk south past the Tithe Barn and continue until you reach the junction with the old Coach Road. The collapsed control shelter sits in the corner of the field immediately in front of you and, although overgrown, can be identified by the emergency exit metal ladder emerging from the undergrowth.

Wilmington Airfield is just north of the A27 road between Lewes and Eastbourne. Park in the lay-by opposite Milton Street and follow the 'Wealdway' north; the hangar is amongst the buildings on the left side. Follow the footpath north some 300m to find the pillbox, which sits on a field boundary.

References/Background reading

Brooks, R.J. 1996, 'Wilmington Airfield', *Sussex Express*, 9 August, 13
Dobinson, C. 2000, *Fields of Deception*, London, Methuen Publishing Ltd

SITE 44: HAILSHAM

Period:　　**Second World War**
Type of site:　　**Nodal Point**

History

Hailsham was designated a Nodal Point and put into a state of defence in the summer of 1940. A line of anti-tank cubes was constructed around the inner town, filling the gaps between houses to form a continuous perimeter, whilst roadblocks formed from coffins and hairpin rails were located at all of the entry points. Civil Defence organisations were established in the town and a number of air-raid shelters constructed. The 20th Sussex (Hailsham) Home Guard Battalion was raised in the town and surrounding villages.

Green Brothers, an engineering company, situated in Western Road was involved in the production of full-size replica Hurricanes, which were used as decoys on airfields and at dummy airfield sites.

Construction of the Hailsham bypass (now the A22) had just been started and was left unfinished when war broke out. To cover the newly constructed bridge over the River Cuckmere two machine gun emplacements were built, one being located on either side of the road. The surrounding fields were covered with anti-glider posts and wires. Interestingly a surviving defence scheme shows the bridge with a roadblock, covered by two anti-tank guns, but does not show the machine gun emplacements being used.

Michelham Priory, located some 3km to the west of Hailsham, was used as a headquarters by 5th Canadian Infantry Brigade and then later by 8th Canadian Infantry Brigade. Officers were housed in the Priory itself, whilst other ranks were quartered at Crossways House in Upper Dicker village.

The sites today

There is no surviving above-ground evidence for the anti-tank cubes or roadblocks in Hailsham, however a line of around 32 parch marks (*67*) can often be seen in very dry weather running north–south across Hailsham Recreation Ground (TQ 5872 0943).

At Horsebridge there is a single machine gun emplacement covering the A22 bridge over the River Cuckmere (*colour plate 23*). The concrete emplacement is situated in a field to the north-east of the bridge (TQ 5747 1106) and was originally partly sunken with only the upper part visible above ground. It has a protected entrance, with steps down to a square sump in front of the door.

67 A line of parch marks shows up in very dry weather running north–south across Hailsham Recreation Ground. These mark the location of a line of anti-tank cubes that formed the perimeter of the Nodal Point. *Copyright: Peter Hibbs*

There are five long narrow embrasures providing an almost 360° field of fire. A second similar emplacement was located on the north-west side of the bridge (approximately TQ 572109), but this was demolished after the war.

At Michelham Priory (TQ 5585 0934) there is little surviving evidence for its use during the war, although a platform behind the dovecote may indicate the site of one or two Nissen huts. In the Gatehouse there is a wartime map of France on the first floor, probably used to follow the progress of allied forces after D-Day, and some wartime graffiti at the top of the stairs to the roof. Close to the entrance are four anti-tank buoys lining the verge (TQ 5578 0942), with another four in the adjacent farm car park. Crossways House is now part of St Bede's School.

At Horam, to the north of Hailsham, there are two pairs of loopholes crudely cut through a brick wall covering the adjacent road junction (TQ 5771 1736).

Directions and access

The Horsebridge machine gun emplacement is on private land, but can be seen from the A22 and a footpath to the north-east.

Michelham Priory is owned by Sussex Archaeological Society and is signposted from the A22 at Lower Dicker or Hailsham (see below). There is a small museum inside the Priory, which includes information on its wartime role.

The Horam loopholes are in the boundary wall of the Merrydown Cider centre, at the top of a steep bank. Turn off the A267 into the B2203 and park; walk back to the road junction to view them from the opposite side of the road.

Opening times
Michelham Priory: 01323 844224

Open Tuesday-Sunday, 1 March-31 October (also open on bank holiday Mondays and every Monday during August); March and October: 10.30am-4.30pm; April-July and September: 10.30am-5pm; August: 10.30am-5.30pm

References/Background reading

Farebrother, G. (ed.) 1986, *Hailsham at War*, Falmer, CCE, University of Sussex

www.sussexpast.co.uk

SITE 45: HADLOW DOWN TO STONEGATE

Period: **Second World War**
Type of site: **Pillboxes**

History

Although the GHQ Stop Line had stopped following the River Uck near Buxted (Site 35), pillboxes were constructed to cover bridges across the Uck further east and to continue following the defence line to join up with the River Rother, which rose at Mayfield. From here they follow the River Rother through to Stonegate and beyond. Unlike the contiguous line of defence works along the River Ouse, those along the Rother were positioned to cover the bridges, with both Type 24 and Type 28 pillboxes being utilised. The bridges themselves had roadblocks and anti-tank coffins, whilst the river appears to have been modified in places to improve its ability to act as an anti-tank ditch.

Mayfield was designated as a Nodal Point in 1940 as it occupied a dominating position on the high ground in the Weald, with an important road from Heathfield to Tunbridge Wells running through the village from south to north. Some pillboxes were also positioned to cover the approaches to Mayfield from the south-west.

The sites today

From Howbourne Farm (Site 35) eastwards, pillboxes were situated to cover crossing points over the River Uck. The first of these is at Hastingford Farm (TQ 5236 2583). This is a 'squashed' Type 24, and is situated on the east side of the road, facing south to cover the bridge. According to the owner, it originally had a timber and wire netting structure on its roof, which was covered with straw to resemble a haystack. Inside there are four embrasures, below which is an extant wooden shelf sitting on brick supports. Outside there was a brick blast wall, although much of this has been demolished. Further east is a similar 'squashed'

68 A Type 24 pillbox, with a detached blast wall protecting its entrance, situated east of
Moat Farm, near Mayfield (TQ 5947 2521)

Type 24, sitting in the edge of a wood (TQ 5286 2608) and facing south to
cover a small farm bridge across the River Uck. This one has three preformed-
concrete embrasures, an internal brick blast wall and its metal door is still in
situ. At Huggetts Furnace Farm there is another similar pillbox (TQ 5343 2600)
covering a farm bridge. This pillbox has been modified post-war with a brick
structure and fuel tank added to its roof.

At Holmstall, north of Butchers Cross a line of anti-tank coffins sit astride
the road (TQ 5624 2615), with 10 on the west side and seven on the east side.
An overgrown Type 24 pillbox, with an external blast wall, covers this roadblock
from the garden of 'Holmstall' (TQ 5625 2618). Two pillboxes cover the A267
road as it approaches Mayfield from the south-west, one on each side of the road
(TQ575264 and TQ577262). To the south of Mayfield there are two Type 28A
pillboxes, the first in a field near the sewage works (TQ581254) covering the
railway bridge and the second covering St Dunstan's Bridge in Newick Lane
from a hedgeline to the north-east (TQ 5892 2510). Along Newick Lane there are
10 anti-tank buoys at the entrance to Bungehurst Farm (TQ 5950 2403) and five
outside Clayton's Farm (TQ585256).

A Type 24 pillbox, with a detached blast wall protecting its entrance (*68*),
is situated east of Moat Farm (TQ 5947 2521) and covers a small farm bridge
across the river. Further east in a hedgeline covering Scotsford Bridge is a Type
24 with a detached blast wall (TQ 6025 2539). A pillbox at TQ628260 covers
Turk's Bridge, whilst at Bivelham Forge Bridge there is a Type 28A pillbox
revetted into a bank to the west of the bridge (TQ 6361 2646). This has a 6pdr

69 This Type 24 pillbox sits on the edge of Newbridge Wood at Bivelham Forge Farm (TQ 6461 2680), and covers a small farm bridge across the river. It has five machine gun tables formed from semi-circles of concrete sitting on brick supports

holdfast and its entrance is enclosed by an L-shaped blast wall. On the east side of the road a 'squashed' Type 24 is built into the top of a stream bank (TQ 6377 2650). This pillbox has an internal blast wall and three small embrasures with an in situ wooden shelf sitting on brick supports. There is also an external blast wall protecting the entrance. Three anti-tank buoys line the verge at Pound Bridge (TQ 6330 2646). A Type 24 pillbox sits in the edge of Newbridge Wood at Bivelham Forge Farm (TQ 6461 2680) and covers a small farm bridge across the river. This pillbox has five pre-cast concrete embrasures and inside the machine gun tables are formed from semi-circles of concrete sitting on brick supports (*69*).

At Witherenden Bridge, south of Stonegate, there is a Type 28A pillbox covering the bridge from the north-east (TQ656268). South of the bridge 13 anti-tank buoys line the verge (TQ 6529 2675), whilst a further two lie in the adjacent field.

Directions and access
Many of the pillboxes in this area are on private property and cannot be visited. The following sites are the only ones that can be seen from the road or adjacent footpaths.

The pillbox at Hastingford Farm is visible from the road, although very overgrown. There is a pull-in by the bridge 50m south of the pillbox. The footpath east from Hastingford Cottage passes the 'squashed' Type 24 pillbox in the edge of the wood and takes you on to Huggetts Furnace Farm, where another path brings you back to the road near the lay-by.

The roadblock at Holmstall can be found by taking the minor road to Rotherfield north from the A267 at Butchers Cross. There is no parking at the site, but there is a parking place at the junction with a minor road 200m south of the site. The two Type 24 pillboxes between Moat Farm and Scotsford Bridge are adjacent to the footpath that follows the river; the first is immediately north of a small bridge, whilst the second is hidden in a hedgeline 50m west of Scotsford Bridge.

At Bivelham Forge Bridge the Type 28A pillbox is set into the bank a short way along the footpath to the west of the bridge, whilst the 'squashed' Type 24 is on the footpath to the east of the bridge. Continue along this footpath for about one kilometre, past Bivelham Forge Farm, to find the Type 24 pillbox in the edge of Newbridge Wood. Anti-tank buoys line the verge south of Witherenden Bridge and the Type 28A pillbox can be seen across the fields to the north-east of the bridge, but cannot be visited.

SITE 46: BODIAM AND SALEHURST

Period: **Second World War**
Type of site: **Pillboxes**

History

Bodiam Castle was built in the late fourteen century and was located in an elevated position to command the crossing point over the River Rother. An earthwork platform called 'The Gun Garden' located upslope of the castle at Court Lodge (TQ 7846 2594) has been claimed as a Civil War gun platform, but is in fact an ornamental garden terrace or viewing platform. During 1940 a Type 28A anti-tank pillbox was erected in the north-east corner of the 'Tilt-yard' to cover the bridge over the River Rother. There must have been other defences at the bridge and possibly a second pillbox, but no trace of these survives today.

Pillboxes were also built to cover other bridges over the River Rother between Bodiam and Salehurst. The B2244 crossed the Rother 1.5km to the west of Bodiam and was protected by a Type 28A anti-tank pillbox, together with an unusual circular two-storey pillbox. South of Salehurst, a Type 24 pillbox was placed on the embankment of the dismantled railway line to cover Church Bridge.

Etchingham and Robertsbridge were Category A Nodal Points, whilst Hurst Green and Cooper's Corner were both Category B Nodal Points.

The sites today

The Bodiam Type 28A pillbox is constructed from brick-shuttered concrete and sits on a concrete base set into the bank of the Tilt-yard (TQ 7851 2553).

This has the effect of reducing its profile and with the castle to its rear makes it difficult to see from any distance (*colour plate 24*). It has an external blast wall with a small embrasure and a ramp down to its entrance. Inside it is divided into two compartments. The west compartment has a large embrasure in the south wall with a holdfast for a 6pdr anti-tank gun, together with a small embrasure in the west wall. The eastern compartment has three larger machine gun embrasures, with a continuous wooden table sitting on brick columns below. A small embrasure is located in the rear wall of this compartment. Interestingly, the rear and west walls of the pillbox, which are largely protected by the bank, are much thinner than the other walls.

Just north of the bridge that carries the B2244 over the River Rother is an unusual two-storey circular pillbox (*70*). It is situated on the east side of the road, with a small stream on its north side (TQ 7705 2477). The protected entranceway is on the north side, with the entrance itself being below ground level. On the ground floor there are five small embrasures and a blast wall. A hole in the ceiling, which presumably originally had a ladder, leads to the first floor. This floor also has five embrasures each having a semi-circular concrete table. The pillbox is constructed from brick-shuttered concrete and has a concrete roof with an edging course of diagonally placed bricks. Unfortunately this unique pillbox has suffered recent fire damage and is frequently flooded. On the west side of the B2244 road and close to some farm buildings, is a Type 28A pillbox (TQ 7689 2452). It is situated on the west bank of a stream and faces south-east to cover the

70 An unusual two-story circular pillbox covers a bridge over the River Rother near Bodiam (TQ 7705 2477)

bridge. It has a large square embrasure, chamfered front corners and a blast wall protecting its entrance on the north-east side.

The brick-shuttered Type 24 pillbox situated south of Salehurst has five prefabricated embrasures, with a semi-circular concrete table below each one. This pillbox originally had a false chimney on its roof as part of its camouflage as a railway ganger's hut. This has now gone and part of the roof has been demolished, which has led to the pillbox being flooded.

Directions and access
Bodiam Castle is located at TQ 7856 2562 and can be reached by turning off the A229 Hawkhurst to Hastings road to Bodiam, and is signposted through the village. The castle is owned by the National Trust and access to the pillbox can be gained when the castle is open. There is a large car park, café and toilets.

The circular pillbox on the B2244 can be seen from the road. It is located just inside a field entrance and can be easily inspected, although there is nowhere to park on this fast road. The Type 28A pillbox is on private property and difficult to see from the road.

To get to the Salehurst pillbox, park at Salehurst Church and follow the footpath south towards Church Bridge. It can be found on the west side of the footpath on the old railway embankment.

Opening times
Bodiam Castle is open from mid-February to October, 10.30am-6.00pm or dusk if earlier, and from November to mid-February, Saturday and Sunday only, 10.30am-4.00pm or dusk if earlier. The castle is closed 24 December-5 January. Last admission is one hour before closing.

Telephone: 01580 830436

References/Background reading
Smith, V. 2000, *The Second World War Pillbox at Bodiam Castle*, Unpublished Report for The National Trust
Thackray, D. 1991, *Bodiam Castle*, London, The National Trust

SITE 47: BATTLE

Period: **Tudor period to the Cold War**
Type of site: **Gun-founding industry, Nodal Point and ROC post**

History
Documentary evidence shows that the Ashburnham furnace near Battle was built prior to 1554 and was one of a large number of blast furnaces operating in

the Sussex Weald at this time. It continued to operate through to the start of its decline in 1763 and its eventual closure in 1813. One of its major products during this time was the founding of cannon, both for the Crown and for sale on the open market. A number of broken cannon moulds have been found at the site.

The furnace was water-powered, using water stored in a large pond to turn a wheel which powered the bellows of the blast furnace. The guns were cast in moulds in circular gun-casting pits and then bored-out to the required internal diameter in a boring-mill, possibly also powered by a water wheel. Documents show that the Ashburnham forge was converted for boring in 1677 and a new boring mill was built in the middle of the eighteenth century. Many cannon produced in the Wealden furnaces are found all over the world, including the West Indies, Mombassa and some of the Mediterranean islands. The only known Sussex-produced cannon to survive in Sussex today is mounted on a modern carriage in Pevensey Castle (Site 18).

Battle was designated a Category A Nodal Point in 1940 and fortified by a ring of anti-tank cubes which encircled the town. These were supported by roadblocks at all the entry points to the town, whilst a number of pillboxes and defensive positions were constructed. Battle Abbey was taken over by the Army during the war and used as a hospital. Ninfield was also designated at a Nodal Point.

The ROC monitoring post at Ninfield was opened in January 1962 and closed in September 1991. It comprised an underground monitoring post, with an adjacent two-storey observation tower.

The sites today

Ashburnham has been selected as an example of a cannon-producing blast furnace, as parts of the site can be seen today from the adjacent footpath (TQ 6861171). There were many other similar furnaces operating in the Weald during this period, including those at Robertsbridge, Pippingford, Heathfield and Beckley. Parts of Beckley furnace (TQ836212) and Robertsbridge furnace (TQ 751231) can also be seen from adjacent road and footpaths.

Although most of the Battle Nodal Point installations were removed after the war, a significant stretch of anti-tank cubes survives on the north-east side of the town adjacent to St Mary's Parish Church (71). The line of some 70 cubes commences at the entrance to the Church Hall (TQ 7499 1584), where some run along the rear of gardens to the west of the hall. The main line then extends from the rear of the Church Hall (TQ 7500 1590) and follows the boundary of the Deanery before stopping at the rear of the houses to the east of the Church. On the south-west side of the town a single cube survives (TQ 7460 1603) from a line of at least 16 that were recorded here in 1975, the remainder having been subsequently removed for new houses and shops. A possible pillbox was recorded in 1975 as surviving at TQ749160, disguised to match the wall at the rear of gardens. A recent visit could not confirm this as the site is very overgrown. Numerous anti-tank buoys survive at various sites around the town

71 Anti-tank cubes adjacent to St Mary's Parish Church, Battle (TQ 7499 1584)

and presumably originate from the roadblocks. Seven examples can be found at the entrance to Punch Bowl Farm (TQ 7518 1727) on Whatlington Road to the north of the town and four buoys are situated outside houses on the A2100 to the east of the town (TQ 7655 1484). South-west of the town on the B2204 (Catsfield Road) a closed off lay-by north of Parkgate Manor is lined with 47 anti-tank cylinders (TQ 7247 1472).

A line of almost 100 anti-tank cubes forming the western side of the Ninfield Nodal point can be found in woodland between TQ 6997 1299 and TQ 6981 1279. The ROC post at Ninfield is located on the north-east corner of the Ninfield reservoir. The brick-built observation post is boarded up and very overgrown. It is surrounded by a wire fence, which also encloses the adjacent underground monitoring post. A trig point on the top of the reservoir is dedicated to '203 Ashburnham Patrol of the British Resistance Movement 1940-44'.

Directions and access

To get to Ashburnham Forge, take the A269 from Battle, then turn onto the B2204. After 0.5km, turn right onto a minor road. Park at Ashburnham Forge and follow the public footpath north to Furnace Cottage. The furnace site is on the east side of the footpath.

The sites in Battle are best found on foot, having parked in one of the car parks in the town centre. St Mary's Church Hall is off Upper Lake, just to the east of Battle Abbey, and a footpath takes you past the Church Hall to see the cubes at its rear. Another path takes you back towards the car parks and past the possible pillbox.

The single cube can be found along Western Avenue off the High Street, and close to Battle Museum. It is hidden in a hedge on the right side, beside a seat.

The anti-tank cubes at Ninfield can be seen from Combe Lane. Ninfield ROC post is at the reservoir, which is on the north side of the High Street and marked by a large water tower. Access was possible until recently from the footpath alongside Cookstown Close, but this has now been closed off, and public access to the reservoir is not permitted.

References/Background reading

Cleere, H. and Crossley, D. 1995, *The Iron Industry of the Weald*, Cardiff, Merton Priory Press Ltd

King, P.W. 1995, 'Ashburnham furnace in the early 18th century', *Sussex Archaeological Collections* 133, 255-62

www.subbrit.org.uk/cgi-bin/webdata_roc.pl

SITE 48: PEVENSEY LEVELS AND WARTLING

Period: **Second World War to the Cold War**
Type of site: **Radar stations, pillboxes and anti-tank obstacles**

History

The low ground of the Pevensey Levels and Wartling made an ideal location for some of the early radar stations that played such a decisive role in the Battle of Britain. The RAF Pevensey Chain Home radar station at Manxey Level (TQ643072) was built in 1939 and served throughout the war, being finally put on care and maintenance in December 1945. The radar station was spread over a large area incorporating the transmitter and receiver blocks and masts, administration buildings and accommodation. The two approach roads from the south were both guarded by Type 25 pillboxes.

RAF Wartling was a GCI radar station located a short distance east of RAF Pevensey (TQ654075) and became operational in 1941. The GCI station was located on the east side of the Wartling Road and eventually had a large operations block, called a 'Happidrome', and a single Type 7 rotating aerial array. The station was defended by a number of pillboxes. The domestic site for the GCI station was located north of Wartling village in Plantation Wood (TQ654107).

RAF Wartling continued to be used after the war and with the advent of the atomic bomb it was decided in 1950 that the operations room should be underground. However, the existing site would have been liable to flooding so an alternative location was found on the higher ground to the north (TQ662088). Construction of the GCI ROTOR radar station commenced in 1951/2 and was completed in 1955, becoming operational in March of that year. After a number of upgrades, including the installation of a Type 80 radar and modulator building in 1957, the station finally closed in December 1964 and was placed on care and maintenance. The domestic camp for the ROTOR station was located at Barnhorne near Bexhill (TQ697081).

The bridges at Rickney over the Yotham, one of the major watercourses draining the Pevensey Levels, were crucial to the defence of this area as they provided the only means of exit on the north-west side of the Levels. The bridges were turned into a defended locality in the Second World War by the construction of a number of anti-tank cubes and roadblocks. A pillbox or gun emplacement may also have been situated near the two bridges. Later in the war the bridge carrying the road to Hankham was destroyed by a German bomb.

The sites today

Many elements of the RAF Pevensey site still remain today near Pylons Farm, although some structures have been demolished. The original concrete road runs through the site and past the Air Ministry wardens' houses (now renamed Pylons Cottages). The receiver block, some of the tower bases, the buried reserves and some air-raid shelters survive. Two Type 25 pillboxes protecting the southern approaches to the radar station can be seen. The first at TQ 6369 0687 is situated in the corner of a field behind a ditch and covers the south-western road to the site (72). It is partly sunken, and still retains some of its corrugated iron shuttering on the roof interior. The second Type 25 pillbox covers the Wartling Road and the south-eastern approach to the site (TQ 6510 0680). It is also partly sunken and is located behind a ditch. A short distance away is a large section of concrete pipe sunk into the ground that may have been used as a sentry post.

Very little survives of RAF Wartling. The Happidrome was demolished and most of the site was cleared after the new ROTOR station was commissioned. Adjacent to some farm buildings is an unusual square pillbox, similar to a Type 26, with three small oval embrasures and a protected entrance porch (TQ 6531 0748). Close to this is the brick-built No. 1 Interrogator (IFF) building (TQ 6532 0747) (73). A little further from the road are some other surviving structures (approximately TQ654074) and two pillboxes, one of which has an anti-aircraft annex. A small brick building with its metal door survives in situ south of the radar station (TQ 6503 0677) and may be a pyrotechnic store. There is little to see of the domestic site in Plantation Wood apart from the concrete road and a large pile of concrete rubble. A number of concrete boundary posts, with 'WO' and a RN anchor along the side of the road here, are probably associated with Herstmonceux Castle. Others can be found near the entrance to the castle.

The Wartling ROTOR site was sold in 1976, with the Guardhouse being converted into a private house, and more recently the Type 80 modulator building has also been converted into a dwelling. Within the perimeter fence and alongside the approach road, the intake ventilator tower and emergency exit is still extant (TQ 6615 0868). Remote transmitter and receiver blocks were built near

72 Partly sunken Type 25 pillbox on the south-western approach road to the RAF Pevensey radar site (TQ 6369 0687)

73 RAF Wartling. In the foreground is the No. 1 Interrogator (IFF) building (TQ 6532 0747), with concrete bases for its associated mast. To its rear is one of the pillboxes defending the site

Hooe, the transmitter being at TQ 6900 1040 and the receiver at TQ 6806 0972. Both have been converted into houses. The domestic site at Barnhorne became a prison (HMP Northeye) and then more recently a training establishment, with very few of the original buildings remaining.

The main group of five anti-tank cubes at Rickney are located on the west bank of the Yotham, immediately to the north of the bridge (TQ 6269 0693), with a further two in the garden of Bridge Farm. At Rickney Farm there are a further six cubes, two on the north side of the road and four on the south side, incorporated into later farm buildings. Their position and spacing suggest that these might also be in their original position. Between these two sets of blocks are three anti-tank buoys arranged along the north verge of the road opposite the farmhouse, whilst alongside the farmhouse are four unusual small-domed concrete blocks. A plaque on the Hankham Bridge tells us it was rebuilt in 1950.

Directions and access

The RAF Pevensey site can be seen from the byeway between Buck's Bridge on the Wartling Road and the minor road from Chilley Green to Rickney. A Type 25 pillbox is located at the latter junction, where it is possible to park. There is no public access to the site itself. The second Type 25 pillbox is on the Wartling Road, with the pyrotechnic store almost directly opposite. Parking is difficult here. The pillbox and No. 1 IFF building at RAF Wartling are the only structures that can be easily seen from the road. There is no public access to any part of this site. To find the remains of the domestic site in Plantation Wood, it is best to park in the large lay-by close to the entrance to Herstmonceux Castle and walk along the road to the site where a public footpath provides access.

To find the ROTOR site, park near the Lamb Inn in Wartling and follow the footpath past the Inn to Court Lodge Farm. Note the anti-tank cylinders here (TQ 6587 0906). Continue along the footpath and the converted Type 80 modulator building (now called Radar House) can be seen on the hilltop. There is no public access to the site.

To get to Rickney from the A27, take the minor road to Wartling from the Pevensey roundabout. After some 200m turn left into a narrow lane and follow this past Chilley Farm (note the anti-tank cylinders on the verge a short distance after the Farm) and past the Type 25 pillbox guarding the entrance to RAF Pevensey. Park in the small lay-by by the bridge at Rickney and walk across the bridge to find the cubes.

References/Background reading

Longstaff-Tyrrell, P. 1998, *A Sussex Sunset, Polegate*, Gote House Publishing

www.subbrit.org.uk/sb-sites/sites/p/pevensey_chain_home/index.shtml
www.subbrit.org.uk/rsg/sites/w/wartling/index.html
www.subbrit.org.uk/rsg/sites/w/wartling_big_pump/index.html

SITE 49: CRIPP'S CORNER

Period: **Second World War**
Type of site: **Nodal Point**

History

Cripp's Corner was designated as a 'fortress' in 1940 and subsequently a Nodal Point owing to the system of roads that radiated out from the village. A perimeter comprising some 800 anti-tank cubes was erected in a single line around the Nodal Point, making good use of the existing woods and sunken roads wherever possible. Roadblocks were placed across the roads where they cut through the perimeter and these were additionally protected by pillboxes and fortified buildings. The construction of the defences was carried out by 205th Field Company RE in August and September 1940, assisted by civilian contractors.

The site today

A substantial part of the original defences survives at Cripp's Corner, with long sections of the line of anti-tank cubes still in situ (*colour plate 25*). On the west side of the village at Swaile's Green, some 128 cubes survive on the north side of the B2089, incorporated into the field boundaries (TQ 7718 2105-TQ 7727 2123). On the south side of the B2089 there are five cubes at the end of the lane to Footlands Farm (TQ 7717 2099). Further down the sunken lane the cubes start again on the east side and then head off to Kemp's Wood (TQ 7720 2089 to TQ 7734 2081).

74 Anti-tank cubes on the northern side of the Cripp's Corner Nodal Point. The examples form the corner between the B2244 and Upper Morgay Wood

75 This small regular trapezium pillbox has three embrasures covering the road and the line of cubes adjacent to the B2244 at Cripp's Corner (TQ 7755 2124). It is currently used as the base for a garden shed

To the north of the village, 45 cubes line the east side of the B2244. Starting on the high ground close to the flyover, they follow the road for about 100m and then turn east to follow the field boundary (74) where a further 32 cubes line the field edge to Upper Morgay Wood (TQ 7762 2123-7774 2133). Close to the start of this line at the flyover, there is a small variant pillbox built into the roadside bank (TQ 7755 2124). This pillbox is a regular trapezium shape and has three embrasures covering the road and the line of cubes. It is in good condition and is currently used as the base for a garden shed (75).

On the east side of the village the line of cubes runs for a short distance alongside the B2089, but then heads north following field boundaries in a zigzag, until it reaches a footpath where it turns west along the reservoir to the B2165 (TQ 7806 2105-TQ 7808 2149). Some 300 cubes form this part of the line, but there is no surviving trace of any roadblocks or pillboxes here, although a pillbox was possibly located at TQ780213.

To the south of Cripp's Corner the line of anti-tank cubes (76) stretches from Thorp's Wood, following field boundaries to the B2244 (TQ 7791 2046-TQ 7767 2039), where there is another variant pillbox. This is an irregular trapezium shape and sits in the corner of the field (TQ 7767 2039), with its entrance on the road side and its three embrasures covering the line of cubes to the east and the ground to the south. The line of cubes turns north here and follows the road for a short distance to TQ 7766 2047. There is no trace of a roadblock here, but the line of cubes continues on the west side of the B2244 along the side of the lane

76 Anti-tank cubes on the southern perimeter of the Cripp's Corner Nodal Point showing how the cubes were integrated into existing hedgelines

to the vineyard and then on to Kemp's Wood (TQ 7764 2047-TQ7763 2039). One cube in this line has the date '1940' inscribed on it. Close to the B2244 and alongside the lane to the vineyard, the cubes pass a brick rectangular building, which is windowless apart from a single loophole facing west along the lane (TQ 7764 2037). This structure is obviously of Second World War date, but its original function here on the perimeter is unclear.

There are a number of anti-tank buoys in the area around Cripp's Corner and there are 12 anti-tank cylinders at the Council Depot on the B2089 (TQ 7822 2087).

Directions and access

Various sections of the line can be viewed from vantage points and adjacent paths and roads. At Swaile's Green there is a small lay-by for parking and the cubes to the north of the road can be viewed from here or the adjacent lane. Crossing the road the five cubes at the end of the lane to Footland Farm can be seen, whilst a few others are visible further down the lane. To see the line of cubes to the north of the village, it is best to park in the village centre, near to the garage where there is a lay-by on the B2089, and with care walk out along the B2244. The pillbox here is in the private garden of a house and cannot be seen from the road. To view the line of cubes to the east of the village, park in the lay-by opposite the Council Depot and walk up Beacon Lane where occasional glimpses can be seen of the cubes, then turn left onto the footpath that leads to the B2165 and past the reservoir, which takes you along part of the line.

To the south, there is a lay-by south of the vineyard on the B2244. Walk back to the line of cubes, where a footpath takes you past the pillbox and line of cubes to the east of the road. A footpath also takes you to the vineyard, past the brick building and on to Kemp's Wood.

References/Background reading

Foot, W. 2006a, *Beaches, fields, streets and hills: the anti-invasion landscapes of England*, CBA Research Report 144, York, Council for British Archaeology

Foot, W. 2006b, *The Battlefields That Nearly Were*, Stroud, Tempus Publishing Ltd

Martin, R. 1999, *Report on Anti-tank Defences around Cripp's Corner in the Parishes of Ewhurst and Sedlescombe*, Unpublished Report

SITE 50: BALDSLOW AND BREDE

Period: **Second World War to Cold War**
Type of site: **Nodal Point and underground bunkers**

History

Baldslow is located to the north of Hastings and was selected as a Category A Nodal Point due to its position at an important road junction. The defences were constructed using local contractors between July and October 1940. The Nodal Point was encircled by a single line of anti-tank cubes, with roadblocks placed at each of the entry points. There were at least two pillboxes together with a number of fortified buildings and a fixed flame defence.

Beauport Park was used as a base by Canadian troops later in the war, with the house being used as an Officer's Club and Divisional headquarters and the surrounding woodland providing cover for ammunition and other stores. An Auxiliary Unit underground out-station radio site was located in Ring Wood to the west of Beauport Park Golf Course.

A nuclear bunker was constructed at the Brede Waterworks (TQ 8144 1784) a few miles north of Baldslow, in the early 1990s. It was intended to house up to 50 personnel who would manage utility services in the event of a regional emergency for up to three months.

The sites today

Some parts of the anti-tank cube line at Baldslow survive today, although most of the defence works were removed after the war. The best surviving evidence is in the garden of 'My Way Lodge', where 28 cubes survive in a line (77) running east–west (TQ 7980 1336–TQ 7974 1338). Further uprooted cubes can be seen in the adjacent grounds of Beauport Park. The line originally extended to the east into Beauport Park and then turned south, possibly following the line of the current footpath. The cubes here were removed when the reservoir was

77 The line of 28 anti-tank cubes running east–west in the garden of 'My Way Lodge', part of the Baldslow Nodal Point

built in 1969/70. The southern part of the line can be picked up where the footpath enters the recreation ground in Harrow Lane (TQ 7988 1298); the buried roots of three cubes can be seen in the bank beside the path. The line then turned north and crossed the B2093, where it can be seen again with three cubes surviving behind the 'Tile Joint' and another uprooted in its car park (TQ 7997 1312).

Also in the grounds of 'My Way Lodge' is a variant pillbox, which has been converted into a store and covered over by a patio. It was originally sunken and had steps down to an entrance on its south side, with three embrasures facing west, north and east; the west one has a brick table surviving below it.

To the north of Baldslow, at Westfield, there are a number of anti-tank buoys, including two at the entrance to 'Whitegates' on the A28 (TQ 8107 1488), four at the entrance to Church Place Farm and another two at the war memorial by the adjacent church (TQ 8099 1518).

The nuclear bunker at Brede was commissioned in December 1992, but does not appear to have ever been fully equipped (78). It has a double entrance, beyond which are decontamination showers and a generator room. There is then an airlock which provides access into the main bunker. The bunker includes dormitories, a kitchen, toilets and administration rooms, one of which also has an escape shaft hatch. There is also a Faraday Cage, designed to shield communications equipment from the electro-magnetic pulse of a nuclear explosion.

78 The entrance to the Brede Cold War bunker at Brede Waterworks (TQ 8144 1784)

On the A2100 between Baldslow and Battle is an unusual sunken circular pillbox (TQ 7837 1359). It is made from concrete and has a domed concrete roof, with an entrance on its west side and narrow embrasures on the east and south-east sides. This is a unique type of pillbox, being much larger than a typical Type 25, and was located to cover the road into Battle.

Directions and access

Baldslow is at the junction of the A21 and A2100, to the north of Hastings. The surviving anti-tank cubes at 'My Way Lodge' and the 'Tile Joint' are on private property and cannot be visited. However, by following footpaths and roads, the perimeter of the Nodal Point defences can still be traced. Beauport Park is now a hotel, golf course and caravan park, and there is no public access.

To find the anti-tank buoys at Westfield, take the A28 (Westfield Lane) north of Baldslow.

The Brede bunker is located at Brede Waterworks and can be found by following the A28 from Westfield and turning left along a small lane just before the Red Lion public house. Follow this lane past the church for about one kilometre to reach the waterworks.

The circular pillbox on the A2100 can be found by parking in the large entranceway to Beauport Park Hotel and walking some 50m west and crossing to the other side of the road. The pillbox is on private property, but can be seen through the gate.

Opening times

The Brede bunker is managed by the Brede Steam Engine Society and is open on the first Saturday of each month between 10.00am and 4.00pm.
Telephone: 01424 882356

References/Background reading

Angell, S. 1996, *The Secret Sussex Resistance*, Midhurst, Middleton Press
Longstaff-Tyrrell, P. 2002, *Barracks to Bunkers*, Stroud, Sutton Publishing Ltd

www.subbrit.org.uk/rsg/sites/b/brede/index.html

SITE 51: IDEN LOCK

Period:	**Napoleonic to the Second World War**
Type of site:	**Royal Military Canal and anti-tank obstacles**

History

The River Rother followed the line of the Royal Military Canal northwards from Rye to Iden where it turned eastwards and the Royal Military Canal headed off to the north around Romney Marsh to Hythe in Kent. A lock was constructed at Iden to connect the two waterways and was completed in 1808, whilst a Military Road followed the route of the canal, allowing for the rapid deployment of troops to any threatened point along the waterway. As the lock was a vulnerable point it was provided with a garrison and officer's accommodation, together with barracks and stables built adjacent to the lock. In 1810 the canal was opened for public use and tolls were collected for use of both the canal and the Military Road. It declined in use during the nineteenth century and the last toll was collected at Iden Lock on 15 December 1909.

During the Second World War pillboxes were placed along the canal to cover the crossing points and anti-tank pimples appear to have been placed along the canal to enhance its use as an anti-tank ditch.

The site today

Although Iden Lock has not been used since the 1950s, it survives today almost unchanged from the nineteenth century (TQ 9364 2444). Beside the lock is a building that was originally the officers' accommodation and was later used as the lock keeper's house (79), whilst on the opposite side of the road are the other rank's barracks and stables.

Type 22 pillboxes were originally situated at Boonshill Bridge and at the bridge at Scots Float on the Military Road between Rye and Iden Lock. Both were demolished after the war, but just north of Scots Float there are seven anti-tank pimples between the road and river (TQ 9334 2294).

79 Iden Lock. These buildings formed the officer's accommodation and were later used as the lock keeper's house

Directions and access

Iden Lock is on the Military Road north of Rye. The anti-tank pimples are just north of Scots Float; continue on this road until it crosses the River Rother. Iden Lock is on the right-hand side where there is a very small car park. A noticeboard provides information on the Lock and Royal Military Canal.

References/Background reading

Hutchinson, G. 1995, *The Royal Military Canal: A Brief History*, Hastings, M & W Morgan

www.royalmilitarycanal.com/pages/history.asp

SITE 52: ASHDOWN FOREST

Period:	**Eighteenth century and Second World War**
Type of site:	**Military encampments, tunnels, radio transmitter and pillboxes**

History

A military camp was formed on 1 July 1793 in Broadwater Forest, to the south-west of Tunbridge Wells, and used prior to the troops moving on to Brighton for a drill parade. Another encampment of similar date was established near Camp Hill north of Duddleswell on Ashdown Forest. During both the First and Second World Wars Ashdown Forest was used as a training area.

An underground HQ bunker was constructed in Hargate Forest, off Broadwater Down on the outskirts of Tunbridge Wells. Construction was begun in 1940 by 172 Tunnelling Company RE and it was finished in late 1941. It comprised three buildings above ground, with steep steps leading 50m below ground, from which two tunnels then ran 120yds parallel to one another. Between these tunnels were eight rooms, each about 15yds long. Although two diesel generators and a telephone system were installed, there were continuous flooding problems, and it does not appear to have ever been used, despite local myths linking it to Montgomery.

The broadcasting transmitter at Kings Standing, near Crowborough, was constructed in 1941 and first broadcast in November 1942 during the Torch landings in North Africa. Set up by the Political Warfare Executive and run in conjunction with the BBC, the site operated throughout the rest of the war and continued in use until 1982, before being finally closed down in 1986. The site comprised a number of different transmitters, underground bunkers and other buildings including a transformer house, a power house and cooling tower. Two small circular pillboxes protected the complex.

80 Interior of the entrance to the underground HQ bunker off Broadwater Down, near Tunbridge Wells (TQ 5742 3763). At the end of this entrance passage a flight of steps (now blocked) takes you down into the underground bunker

Protecting the southern approach road (A267) to Tunbridge Wells from Mayfield were a number of pillboxes constructed in 1940.

The sites today

A line of circular earthen mounds with ditches can be found to the north-west of Camp Hill between TQ 4656 2948 and TQ 4680 2924 and then on to TQ458290, and are the field kitchens of the eighteenth-century military encampment. A similar line of circular mounds extends from TQ 5562 3784 to TQ 5572 3771 and from TQ 5585 3752 to TQ 5597 3737 in Broadwater Forest.

A good example of partly filled-in First World War training trenches can be found between TQ473287 and TQ472287, whilst Second World War slit trenches can be found across the forest. Roadblocks onto the training area can be found at TQ 4691 2889 and TQ 4700 2892 near Camp Hill. Firing ranges used in both World Wars can be found at TQ467298 and TQ495291.

All three of the above-ground structures connected to the underground HQ bunker can be found in Hargate Forest (TQ 5742 3763). Each one is L-shaped and built of brick with a concrete roof. Inside there is evidence of a security gate and steps (now blocked) descend to the underground tunnels (*80*).

After its closure the site at Kings Standing was put up for sale, but before the sale could proceed, it was handed over to the Sussex Police and is today used as a training centre. At the entrance to the site the guardhouse is still extant, however many of the other buildings are not used and are in a poor state of repair. Also at the entrance and on the opposite side of the road are a large number of anti-tank pimples (TQ 4724 2910). One group of 26 form a large square, one side of which borders the road. Further pimples can be found along the minor road between Duddleswell Manor and Nutley (TQ 4706 2888-TQ 4515 2889), with 17 lining the side of the road at TQ 4636 2866. However, it is likely that these have all been moved from the entrance to Kings Standing since the war.

A Type 24 pillbox sits on the village green in Frant (TQ 5897 3526) facing south-west, with its entrance and embrasures bricked up. Further south a thin-walled Type 24 is situated on some high ground in woodland overlooking a road junction at TQ 5813 3282.

Directions and access

The underground tunnel entrances are located in woodland off Broadwater Down. A path runs through the wood and the first structure is about 20m from the road, turning right from the path. The second is found by following the same path through the wood for about 100m. To locate the third, return to the road and take the path straight ahead through the wood; it will be seen after about 50m. The field kitchens at Broadwater Forest are difficult to locate, but there are a number of paths through the woods from the small roads that pass through the forest.

Kings Standing is on the B2026 between Duddleswell and Chuck Hatch. There are numerous car parks nearby, although there is no access to the Kings Standing site. To find the field kitchens walk to Camp Hill and take the path to the north-west; the mounds are about 100m downslope to the right of the path.

The pillbox in Frant is on the village green in the centre of the village, whilst the second pillbox is on the west side of the A267 between Frant and Mark Cross, some 2.25km south of Frant.

References/Background reading

Margary, I.V. 1965, 'Military Field Kitchens of the Eighteenth Century', *Sussex Archaeological Collections* 103, 60-6

Martin, R. 2001, 'King's Standing, Crowborough', *Sussex Industrial History* No. 31, Journal of the Sussex Industrial History Society

The Courier 1979 21 December and 28 December issues

ESCC SMR Records: TQ 53 NE50-MES3284 and TQ 42 NE15-MES4563

GLOSSARY

AOP	Air Observation Post
BL	Breech Loading
Caponier	Structure connected to a fortress and placed so that weapons from its embrasures can fire along the fortress ditch
Casemate	Protected structure containing a gun position, or used as barracks
ECB	Emergency Coastal Battery
Embrasure	Small window or opening in defensive work from which weapons can be fired
En-barbette	Raised gun position on a parapet
Flame fougasse	Remote-controlled explosive flame device
GCI	Ground Controlled Interception
Glacis	Cleared area of sloping ground in front of a fortification
HAA	Heavy Anti-Aircraft
LAA	Light Anti-Aircraft
Lunette	Large detached work with flanks and an open ditch
MT	Motor Transport
OP	Observation Post
QF	Quick Firing
QL	Decoy lighting site
RAF	Royal Air Force

RE	Royal Engineers
RFC	Royal Flying Corps
RML	Rifled Muzzle Loader
RNAS	Royal Naval Air Service
ROC	Royal Observer Corps
SF	Starfish (Special Fires) decoy site

BIBLIOGRAPHY

Angell, S. 1996, *The Secret Sussex Resistance*, Midhurst, Middleton Press

Ashworth, R.C.B. 1985, *Action Stations 9. Military airfields of the Central South and South-East*, Wellingborough, Patrick Stephens Ltd

Barnwell, P.S. (ed.), Cocroft, W.D. and Thomas, R.J.C. 2003, *Cold War: Building for Nuclear Confrontation 1946-1989*, Swindon, English Heritage

Beswick, M. 1987, *Bricks for the Martello Towers in Sussex*, Sussex Industrial History 17, 20-7

Beswick, M. 1993, *Brickmaking in Sussex*, Midhurst, Middleton Press

Bilton, D. 2004, *The Home Front in the Great War*, Barnsley, Pen & Sword Books Limited

Brooks, R.J. 1993, *Sussex Airfields in the Second World War*, Newbury, Countryside Books

Buchan Innes, G. 2000, *British Airfield Buildings Vol. 2: The Expansion & Inter-War Periods*, Leicester, Midland Publishing

Buckton, H. 1993, *Forewarned is Forearmed*, Leatherhead, Ashford, Buchan & Enright

Bull, S. 2002, *World War I Trench Warfare (1) 1914-16*, Oxford, Osprey Publishing Ltd

Burgess, P. and Saunders, A. 1990, *Battle over Sussex 1940*, Midhurst, Middleton Press

Burgess, P. and Saunders, A. 1994, *Blitz over Sussex 1941-42*, Midhurst, Middleton Press

Burgess, P. and Saunders, A. 1995, *Bombers over Sussex 1943-45*, Midhurst, Middleton Press

Chamberlain, P. and Gander, T. 1975, *Anti-Aircraft Guns, World War 2 Fact Files*, London, Macdonald & Jane's

Clarke, D. 2005, *British Artillery 1914-19: Heavy Artillery*, Oxford, Osprey Publishing Ltd

Clements, W.H. 1999, *Towers of Strength: Martello Towers Worldwide*, Barnsley, Pen & Sword Books Ltd

Crook, P. 1998, *Sussex Home Guard*, Midhurst, Middleton Press

Dobinson, C. 2000, *Fields of Deception*, London, Methuen Publishing Ltd

Dobinson, C. 2001, *AA Command*, London, Methuen Publishing Ltd

Duffy, C. 1975, *Fire & Stone*, London, David & Charles Ltd

Ellis, C. and Chamberlain, P. (eds) 1975, *Handbook on the British Army 1943*, London, Purnell Book Services Ltd

Evans, M.M. 2004, *Invasion! Operation Sealion 1940*, Harlow, Pearson Education Ltd

Fleming, P. 1957, *Invasion 1940*, London, Rupert Hart-Davis

Foot, W. 2006, *Beaches, fields, streets and hills: the anti-invasion landscapes of England*, CBA Research Report 144, York, Council for British Archaeology

Foot, W. 2006b, *The Battlefields That Nearly Were*, Stroud, Tempus Publishing Ltd

Forty, G. 2000, *British Army Handbook 1939-1945*, London, Chancellor Press

Goodwin, J.E. 1985, *The Military Defence of West Sussex*, Midhurst, Middleton Press

Goodwin, J.E. 1994, *Fortification of the South Coast: The Pevensey, Eastbourne and Newhaven Defences 1750-1945*, Worthing, JJ Publications

Goodwin, J.E. 2000, *Military Signals from the South Coast*, Midhurst, Middleton Press

Grehan, J. 2001, *Battles & Battlefields of Sussex*, Storrington, Historic Military Press

Grieves, K. 2004, *Sussex in the First World War*, Sussex Record Society Volume 84

Harrington, P. 2004, *English Civil War Archaeology*, London, English Heritage/B.T. Batsford

Haythornthwaite, P. 1996, *The English Civil War 1642-1651*, London, Arms & Armour Press

Haythornthwaite, P. 1998, *The Armies of Wellington*, London, Brockhampton Press

Hayward, J. 2001, *The Bodies on the Beach*, Dereham, CD41 Publishing

Henry, C. 2003, *British Napoleonic Artillery 1793-1815 (2) Siege and Coastal Artillery*, Oxford, Osprey Publishing Ltd

Hodgkinson, J.S. 1996, 'The decline of the ordnance trade in the Weald: The seven year's war and its aftermath', *Sussex Archaeological Collections* 134, 155-67

Holgate, R. 1988, 'Further Investigations at the Later Neolithic Domestic Site and Napoleonic 'Camp' at Bullock Down, Near Eastbourne, East Sussex', *Sussex Archaeological Collections* 126, 21-30

Hudson, A. 1984, 'Volunteer Soldiers in Sussex during the Revolutionary and Napoleonic Wars, 1793-1815', *Sussex Archaeological Collections* 122, 165-81

Hudson, A. 1986, 'Napoleonic Barracks in Sussex', *Sussex Archaeological Collections* 124, 267-268

Humphrey, G. 1998, *Eastbourne at War*, Seaford, S.B. Publications

Hutchinson, G. 1995, *The Royal Military Canal: A Brief History*, Hastings, M & W Morgan

Hylton, S. 2004, *Kent and Sussex 1940*, Barnsley, Pen & Sword Books Ltd

Kitchen, F. 1986, 'The Ghastly War-Flame: Fire Beacons in Sussex until the mid 17th Century', *Sussex Archaeological Collections* 124, 179-91

Leslie, K. and Short, B (eds) 1999, *An Historical Atlas of Sussex*, Chichester, Phillimore

Longstaff-Tyrell, P. 1999, *Tyrrell's List*, Polegate, Gote House Publishing

Longstaff-Tyrell, P. 2000, *Front-Line Sussex*, Stroud, Sutton Publishing Ltd

Longstaff-Tyrell, P. 2002, *Barracks to Bunkers*, Stroud, Sutton Publishing Ltd

Longstaff-Tyrell, P. 2004, *Operation Cuckmere Haven*, Polegate, Gote House Publishing

Lower, M.A. 1870, *A Survey of the Coast of Sussex made in 1587*, Lewes?

Lowry, B. (ed.) 1996, *20th Century Defences in Britain: An Introductory Guide*, York, Council for British Archaeology

Lowry, B. 1998, 'Hunting the Survivors of Dad's Army', *British Archaeology* No. 40

Lowry, B. 2004, *British Home Defences 1940-45*, Oxford, Osprey Publishing Ltd

Lowry, B. 2006, *Discovering Fortifications: from the Tudors to the Cold War*, Princes Risborough, Shire Publications Ltd

McCutcheon, C. 2006, *Home Guard Manual 1941*, Stroud, Tempus Publishing Ltd

Mace, M.F. 1997, *Sussex Wartime Relics and Memorials*, Storrington, Historic Military Press

Marsden, P. 1987, *The Historic Wrecks of South-East England*, Norwich, Jarrold & Sons Ltd

Osborne, M. 2004, *Defending Britain*, Stroud, Tempus Publishing Ltd

Pegden, B.K. 1980, 'The Purchase of Bricks for Martello Towers in the Year 1804', Fort Vol. 8, Fortress Study Group

Planel, P. 1995, *A Teacher's Guide to Battlefields Defence Conflict and Warfare*, London, English Heritage

Rowland, D. 2001, *Coastal Blitz*, Seaford, S.B. Publications

Sanders, I.J. 2005, *Pillboxes: Images of an Unfought Battle*, Lightning Source UK Ltd

Saunders, A. 1997, *Channel Defences*, London, English Heritage/B.T. Batsford

Shores, C. 1991, *Fledgling Eagles*, London, Grub Street

Telling, R.M. 1997, *English Martello Towers: A Concise Guide*, Beckenham, CST Books

Vine, P.A.L. 1972, *The Royal Military Canal*, Newton Abbot, David & Charles PLC

Williamson, J.A. 1959, *The English Channel*, London, Collins

Wills, H. 1985, *Pillboxes: A study of U.K. Defences 1940*, London, Leo Cooper

Yarrow, A. 1979, *The Fortifications of East Sussex*, Lewes, ESCC

INDEX

Entries in italics refer to illustrations